PREACHING

A SERMON
COLLECTION

Charles H. Spurgeon

PREACHING

Introduction by JASON K. ALLEN

B&H
PUBLISHING
BRENTWOOD, TENNESSEE

978-1-0877-8448-9

Published by B&H Publishing Group
Brentwood, Tennessee

Dewey Decimal Classification: 251
Subject Heading: SPURGEON, CHARLES
HADDON / PREACHING / PASTORAL
THEOLOGY

All Scripture references are taken from the
King James Version; public domain.

Cover design by B&H Publishing Group.
Cover image by Photo 12 / Alamy Stock Photo.

All Spurgeon sermons used are public domain.

1 2 3 4 5 6 • 28 27 26 25 24

Contents

Introduction

Jason K. Allen

More than any other reason, Charles Haddon Spurgeon has obtained ministerial immortality due to his power in the pulpit. Though he launched sixty-six auxiliary ministries—including orphanages and a pastors' college—it was his pulpit prowess that made him a man among men within the ranks of the clergy.

Spurgeon was a true phenom, one who burst onto the scene as an adolescent preacher, and who soon became known as the "boy preacher of the fens."[1] By age nineteen, he was pastoring the most reputable, nonconformist church in London, setting it on a path for explosive growth.

---

1. Susie Spurgeon and J. W. Harrold, *C. H. Spurgeon's Autobiography: Compiled from His Diary, Letters, and Record* (Pasadena TX: Pilgrim Publications, 1992), 1:318.

Weekly, he preached to the largest Lord's Day crowd assembled anywhere on the globe. People literally flocked to hear Spurgeon preach. Common people desired a seat, VIPs demanded one. As was often said, every tourist in London desired an audience with Queen Victoria and to be in the audience of a Spurgeon sermon.

Adding to his influence, his weekly sermons were transcribed, quickly edited, and then distributed around the world. Spurgeon's pulpit ministry flowed through the tentacles of the British Empire, which then spanned the globe.

What made Spurgeon such a phenom? God's hand of favor clearly rested on this anointed servant, and we can detect why and how that favor showed up in Spurgeon's life and ministry.

Providentially, Spurgeon was imbued with unmatched *natural gifts*. He enjoyed a photographic memory, an encyclopedic knowledge of Scripture, church history and theology, a booming voice, an exceptional stage presence, a heightened wit, and he was a natural wordsmith. He could turn a phrase, leverage the power of analogy, and create unforgettable word pictures. To listen to Spurgeon was to be gripped by him, spellbound by the sermon preached.

Along these lines, Spurgeon sought and enjoyed the *Spirit's anointing* on his ministry. People came to hear him preach, but Spurgeon pointed to prayer as the secret of his success. Spurgeon prayed unceasingly throughout his days. Moreover, the prayers of Spurgeon's congregation constantly undergirded him. He often pointed to their prayers as the secret of his success.

On one occasion D. L. Moody traveled to London and, of course, went to hear Spurgeon preach. Upon Moody's return, one inquirer, eager to get a first-hand account of Spurgeon's pulpit ministry, asked Moody if he heard Spurgeon preach. Moody replied, "yes, but better yet, I heard him pray."[2]

When one surveys the totality of Spurgeon's ministry, *courage* stands out as a hallmark of his preaching. Spurgeon was a man who had something to say, and he said it. Throughout his ministry, Spurgeon did not mince words. He had a prophetic voice, and he leveraged his vast platform to parry threats confronting God's people.

Whether it was the Campbellite Controversy, Hyper-Calvinism, Darwinism, or, later in life, the Downgrade Controversy, Spurgeon joined these battles head on. These controversies cost him dearly, with

---

2. Arnold Dallmore, *Spurgeon* (Chicago, IL: Moody Press, 1984), 77.

the Downgrade Controversy costing him most of all. Yet, from his earliest years in ministry until his last, Spurgeon preached with unflagging courage. Thus, he will not be forgotten because his courage in the pulpit is unforgettable.

Spurgeon's *Christological focus* clearly enhanced his effectiveness in the pulpit. He consistently presented a gospel witness, concluding every sermon by making a dash to the cross. His Christocentric approach to preaching meant that every time he preached, the gospel was proclaimed. This also meant sinners were regularly converted under his ministry.

Last, and most especially, Spurgeon believed in the *power of preaching*. And perhaps here lies the greatest secret of all. Many preachers don't experience God's power in their pulpit ministries because they don't expect to experience it. Spurgeon, on the contrary, never entered the pulpit without expecting the Spirit and the Word to change lives. As Spurgeon famously reflected,

> We want again Luthers, Calvins, Bunyans, Whitefields, men fit to mark eras, whose names breathe terror in our foemen's ears. We have dire need of such. Whence will they come to us? They are the gifts of Jesus Christ to the Church, and will come in due time. He

has power to give us back again a golden age of preachers, and when the good old truth is once more preached by men whose lips are touched as with a live coal from off the altar, this shall be the instrument in the hand of the Spirit for bringing about a great and thorough revival of religion in the land.

I do not look for any other means of converting men beyond the simple preaching of the gospel and the opening of men's ears to hear it. The moment the Church of God shall despise the pulpit, God will despise her. It has been through the ministry that the Lord has always been pleased to revive and bless His Churches.[3]

Thus, as you read this little book, I pray you'll resonate with Spurgeon's assessment. We need such preachers because the church needs such preaching.

So, Lord, may it be. And, dear reader, may the Lord use this book to stir such a flame within you as you read it, and may that flame carry you forth as you minister the Word.

---

3. Charles H. Spurgeon, *The Metropolitan Tabernacle Pulpit* (Pasadena, TX: Pilgrim Publications, 1971), 20:605.

Preach, Preach, Preach Everywhere[4]

"And he said unto them, Go ye into all the world, and preach the gospel to every creature. He that believeth and is baptized shall be saved; but he that believeth not shall be damned."
(Mark 16:15–16)

Before our Lord gave his disciples this commission, he addressed them in tones of serious rebuke. You will observe that, appearing unto the eleven as they sat at dinner, "he upbraided them with their unbelief

4. Published in *Metropolitan Tabernacle Pulpit*, Vol. 15 in 1869 by Charles Spurgeon. This is sermon 900, delivered in 1869, exact date unknown.

and hardness of heart because, they believed not them which had seen him after he was risen." So honorable an estimation did he set upon testimony; so marked a censure did he pronounce upon those who neglected it. The reprimand they received on such an occasion may well serve as a caution to us, for unbelief unfits the Christian for service. It is in proportion to our personal faith in the gospel that we become competent witnesses for teaching it to others. Each one of us who would get credit for sincerity must say with David, "I believed, therefore have I spoken," or else a want of faith of ourselves will effectually deprive our speech of all its power over our fellow men.

There can be little doubt that one reason why Christianity is not so aggressive now as it once was, and exerts not everywhere the influence it had in apostolic times, is the feebleness of our faith in Christ as compared with the full assurance of faith exercised by the men of those days. In vain you hide a timid heart behind a modest face when the attitude we should show and the living force that should constrain us is a bold reliance upon the power of the Holy Spirit and a deep conviction of the might of the truth which we are taught to deliver. Brothers, if there is to be a revival of religion, it must begin at home. Our own souls must first of all be filled with holy faith and burning enthusiasm, and then shall we be strong to do exploits and to win provinces for the scepter of King Jesus.

Having thus made a note upon the context, I want you to refer to a parallel passage in Matthew. There we learn that in delivering this commission our Lord assigned a remarkable reason for it, and one that intimately concerned himself. "All power," he said, "is given unto *me* in heaven and in earth, go *you* therefore and teach all nations" These words were adapted to strengthen the faith of his disciples, of whom it had been just observed that "some doubted." Do you not see the point of this announcement? Jesus of Nazareth, being raised from the dead, tells his apostles that he is now invested with universal supremacy as the Son of Man. Therefore he issues a decree of grace, calling on all people of every clime and kindred to believe the gospel with a promise of personal salvation to each and every one who believes. With such authority is this mandate clothed, and so imperative the duty of all men everywhere to repent, that they who do not believe are threatened with a certain penalty of damnation. This royal ordinance he will have published throughout the whole world, but he enjoins it on all the messengers that those who bear the tidings should be thoroughly impressed with the sovereignty of him who sends them. Let the words then ring in your ears, "Go ye therefore." They sound like the music of that glad acclaim that hails the Redeemer installed with power, holding the insignia of power in his possession, exercising the full rights of legitimate power, and entrusting his disciples with a commission founded on that power, "Go ye into all the world."

Yet another remark before we proceed to the text. The commission we are about to deal with was the last the Lord gave to his disciples before he was taken away from them. We prize greatly the last words of his departing servants, how shall we sufficiently value the parting words of our ascending Master? Injunctions left us by those who have gone to glory have great weight upon our spirits; let obedient lovers of Christ see to it that they act according to the last will and testament, the last desire expressed by their risen Lord.

I claim for my text peculiar attention from every disciple of Jesus, not indeed as if it were a mournful entreaty but rather as a solemn charge. You remember Christ's own parable, "The kingdom of heaven is as a man travelling into a far country, who called his own servants, and delivered unto them his goods."[5] Look at this as the last direction Jesus gives to his stewards before "he went into a far country to receive for himself a kingdom and to return." It seems to me that as

---

5. Matthew 25:14.

when the mantle of Elijah fell upon Elisha, Elisha would have been much to blame if he had not caught it up, so when these words fell from our ascending Savior before the clouds concealed him from the disciples' sight, we ought to take them up with holy reverence. Since he has left them as his parting mantle, they ought to be lovingly cherished and scrupulously obeyed.

Come we, then, to invite your earnest heed to the command the Savior here gives: "Go ye into all the world, and preach the gospel to every creature."[6] It was given to the apostles representatively. They represent the whole body of the faithful. To every converted man and woman this commission is given. I grant you there is a specialty to those gifted and called to surrender themselves wholly to the work of the ministry, but their office in the visible church offers no excuse for the discharge of those functions that pertain to every member of the body of Christ in particular. It is the universal command of Christ to every believer: "Go you into all the world, and preach the gospel to every creature."

---

6. Mark 16:15.

What We Carry to Every Creature: The Gospel

There may be no need, my brothers, for me to tell you what the gospel is, but to complete our subject we must declare it. The "gospel," which is to be told to "every creature," it seems to me is the great truth that "God was in Christ reconciling the world unto himself, not imputing their trespasses unto them" and that he "has committed unto us the word of reconciliation." God has looked in pity upon sinful man. He has sent his Son to take upon himself the nature of man. His Son has come in the flesh. He has wrought out a perfect righteousness by his obedient life. He has died upon the tree, the just for the unjust, that whosoever trusts in him might be forgiven. Then come the gospel's point and barb—believe in him and be baptized, and you shall be saved; reject him, and your peril is imminent, for God declares it, you must be damned.

When we preach the gospel, then, we must declare to the sons of men that they are fallen, they are sinful, and they are lost, but Christ has come to seek and to save that which was lost. That there is in Christ Jesus, who is now in heaven, grace all sufficient to meet each sinner's need, that whosoever believes in him shall be forgiven all his sins and shall receive the Holy Spirit, by which he shall be helped to lead a new life, shall be preserved in holiness, and shall be brought safely to heaven. To preach the gospel is to preach up Christ. It is not, as I believe, to preach any form of church government or any special creed, although both of these may be needful to those who have heard and received the gospel. The first message we have to preach to every creature is that there is a Savior: "Life for a look at the Crucified One, life at this moment" for all who look to him. This is the gospel we have to preach.

Now, what is meant by the word "preach"? I take its meaning in this place to be very extensive. Some can literally preach— that is, act as heralds proclaiming the gospel as the town crier proclaims in the street the message he is bidden to cry aloud. The town crier is, in fact, the world's preacher, and the preacher of the gospel is to be a crier, crying aloud and sparing not the truth of Christ. I do not believe that Christ tells us to go and play the orator to every creature. Such a command would be impracticable to most of us and useless to any of us. Of all the things that desecrate the Sabbath and grieve the Spirit, attempts at high-flown oratory and gorgeous eloquence in preaching I believe are about the worst. Our business is just to speak out the gospel simply and plainly to every creature. We do not actually preach the gospel to a man if we do not make him understand what we are talking about. If our language does not come down to his level, it may be the gospel, but it is not the gospel to him. The preacher should adopt language suitable to all his congregation—in preaching he should strive to instruct, to enforce, to explain, to expound, to plead, and to bring home to every man's heart and conscience, as in the sight of God, as far as his ability goes, the truth that beyond all argument or cavil has the seal and stamp of divine revelation.

Though all the members of a church cannot literally preach in this ordinary acceptation of the term, yet if this command be for all, then must all bear that testimony to the world in some other outspoken manner. Their preaching may be in divers ways. Some must preach by their holy lives. Others must preach by their talking to the ones and twos, like the Master at the well, who was as much preaching when he conversed with the woman of Samaria as when he addressed the multitude on the banks of the lake of Gennesaret and uttered doctrine as sublime in that little village of Sychar as he proclaimed at the beautiful gate of the temple. Others must preach by distributing the truth printed for circulation, and a right noble service this is, especially when the pure word of life, the Bible itself, is sown broadcast in this and other lands. If we cannot speak with our own tongue, we must borrow other men's tongues, and if we cannot write with our own pens, we must borrow other men's pens, but we must do it in some way or other.

The gist of this command is that we must make the gospel known to every creature by some means or other—throw it in his way, make him know that there is a gospel, and challenge his very curiosity to learn what it means. You cannot make him accept it or believe it—that is God's work—but you can and must make him know of it and plead with him to receive it, and do not let it be your fault if he does not welcome it. Do all, as much as within you lies, to make every creature know what the gospel is, so that if he will not accept it yet he shall have had the kingdom of God brought nigh to him. The responsibility of his accepting or rejecting it shall then be his business and none of yours. This, then, is the commission of Jesus Christ to his disciples: "Go you into all the world, and preach the gospel to every creature."

Lest we should make a mistake about what I just now called the point and barb of the arrow, the force and pith of the gospel, Christ has put it in plain words, "He that believes and is baptized shall be saved." That is to say, if a man would participate in the bounteous salvation Christ has wrought, he must believe in Christ, he must trust Christ, he must believe Christ to be God's appointed Savior and to be able to save him.

He must act on that belief and trust himself in the hands of Jesus, and if he does that he shall be saved.

Further, the text says he must be baptized. Not that there is any virtue whatsoever in baptism, but it is a small thing for Christ to expect that the man trusting to be saved by him should own and avow his attachment to him. He who wishes to have Christ as his Savior should be prepared openly to acknowledge that he is on Christ's side. Baptism thus becomes the badge of discipleship, the outward token of inward faith by which a man says to all who look on, "I confess myself dead to the world. I confess myself buried with Christ. I declare myself risen to newness of life in him. Make what you will of it and laugh at it as much as you like, yet in the faith of Jesus as my Lord, I have taken leave of all else to follow him." It is a point of obedience.

Sometimes one has said in his heart, "What a pity it is that baptism should have been introduced into this place; it makes a baulk of wood into which men may drive their ritualistic hook." But then the Son of God himself has put it here, and we cannot alter it. If it were not here, I would not have put it here, but it is here, and being here, it is at your soul's hazard, man, to leave it out. I believe with all my heart that if you believe in Jesus Christ you will be saved, whether you are baptized or not, but I would not like to run the risk, mark you, for I have not got that in my text. It is,

"He that believes and is baptized shall be saved," and I would take the two commands together, and obey my Master's will throughout, and not leave out that which did not suit my inclination and accept only that which did. I am bound to leave out neither of them but to take the two together. With your heart you must believe and with your mouth make confession, and if you do, these sincerely you shall be saved.

The Extent of the Commission

Having, then, clearly before us what our work is—to publish and make plain to every creature the gospel of Jesus Christ—let us solemnly consider (for it is a very solemn business, being incumbent upon every professor of Christ here) what the extent of this commission is.

Judging from the fact that there is no mention made of time, I gather that as long as there is a church in the world the obligation to preach the gospel will remain, and if that church should ever come to consist of but one or two, it must still, with all its might, go on promulgating the gospel of Jesus Christ. Preaching is to be for all time, and until Jesus Christ himself shall come and the dispensation shall close, the mission of the church is to go into all the world—all of you—and tell out the gospel to every creature.

I will not, however, dwell upon that, because it is not so much a practical point, but just notice that there is no limit as to where this gospel is to be preached. It is to be preached in "all the world"—in Labrador, in Africa, where the Southern Cross shines high, or where Arcturus with his suns leads on the night. Everywhere, in every place; no nation is to be left out because too degraded; no race is to be forgotten because too far remote. The mission of the church deals with the center of Africa, with men who have never yet looked the pale man in the face. It deals with learned nations, as the acute and skeptical Hindu, and with the degraded tribes, as the Hottentot in his kraal, the Bechuana, and the Bushman. There is to be no omission anywhere. Our great Commander's marching orders to his troops are to "Go ye into all the world, and preach the gospel to every creature."

Even this is not so practical a point as the one I want to insist upon. It is the duty of the church, according to this command, to make known the gospel to every creature. Any one of you individually, of course, cannot make it known to every creature, but each one, at home and abroad, according to his sphere of action and his capacity, is to be striving at that. As soon as ever they can understand, you are to be ready with this gospel of Jesus Christ for them. The Sunday school does not want a direct text for its institution or foundation. It is a marvel that it was not instituted long before it was, for the very spirit of Sabbath school work lies in the words here—"every creature." You are not, in looking after the children, to include only some privileged classes and exclude the ragged and the depraved. The city Arab is at least a "creature," and you are as much bound to preach the gospel to him as to your own dear child, who is the object of your tenderest love. It is to every creature.

Then the Christian church ought to aim at the rich. The rich want the gospel, perhaps, more than any other class in the community. They seldom hear it, and what they do hear of the gospel is poor diluted stuff. Their sins are not often told them to the face, neither are they rebuked as the poor are. They are to be sought for by the church, and though it is difficult to get at them, yet we have not done our duty till we have done what we can for them. But the poor are to be looked after. Their poverty must never make us say that it is not worthwhile to teach them. It is the glory of the gospel that the poor should have the gospel preached to them. Rich and poor are both creatures, and therefore the church has its duty concerning both.

The gospel ought to be preached to those who habitually assemble on the Sabbath. It is a pleasure to remember that there are so many who are willing to come and listen to the gospel, but the responsibility of the minister and the church does not end with those who voluntarily congregate within four walls. We are to preach the gospel to every creature, therefore to those who lie in bed on Sunday mornings, to those who read Sunday newspapers, to those who take their walks in the evening with listless indifference, to those who do not know, perhaps, what Christian worship means. You have not done what your Master has told you to do till you have reached them and made them know, forced them to know, what the gospel is. He would be a poor sportsman who should sit in his house and expect the game to come to him. He that would have it must go abroad for it, and he that would serve the Master must go out into the highways and hedges and compel them to come in.

I need not say here, brothers, that I hope the Christian church is now alive to looking after every class of society, but what I want to bring home personally to ourselves is just this: that we, as a church here, with so many advantages, so many in numbers, have at least a part in this commandment and must extend our efforts to as many of "every creature" as we can. Oh! We cannot discharge the work for which God has put us here until we have looked into these alleys, these lanes, these courts, these dark places and have tried our best to take Jesus Christ's gospel to every dweller therein. I know you have your Sunday schools, and I am thankful you are doing your work there, but do not confine your aspirations to that class. I know I have with this congregation work enough; still I am not bound to limit myself to any parish or to any locality, but if I can, to do good, as much as lies in me in all directions and in all manner of places to make known the gospel to every creature. Have you been the means of the conversion of fifty? That is not "every creature," press on. Were there a hundred added to this church the other day? That is not "every creature." There are millions yet to whom Christ is not known. Preach the gospel everywhere then.

The majesty of this command overwhelms one. Such a commission was never given before or since. O church of God! Your Lord has given you a work almost as immense as the creation of a world. Nay, it is a greater work than that; it is to re-create a world. What can you do in this? You can do nothing effectively unless the Holy Spirit shall bless what you attempt to do. But that he will do, and if you do gird up your loins, and your heart be warm in this endeavor, you shall yet be able to preach Jesus Christ to every creature under heaven.

I must not enlarge, for time flies too quickly. It will suffice if I have put that thought into your hearts, that to the servant girl and the duchess, the chimney sweep and the peer, the man in the poor house or in the palace, we must account ourselves debtors for Christ's sake to present the gospel to them according to our ability, never limiting the sphere of our enterprise where an opportunity can be found to carry the gospel to every creature.

Inducements to Enlist in This Service and Obey the Command

It shall be sufficient answer to many of you to say that the reason for preaching the gospel to every creature is that God has said it. Oh, it was a grand shout—if it had been for a better purpose—when the hundreds of thousands gathered together listening to the burning eloquence of the hermit, when he bade them charge home against the Saracens and deliver the holy sepulcher and the sacred places from the infidel. Then the shout went up, *Deus vult*, "God wills it," and in the strength of that belief, that God willed it, "a forest huge of spears was couched," ten thousand swords were unsheathed, and men dashed on to battle and to death.

Oh! If the Christian church could but feel *Deus vult*, "God wills it," that now, even in this year of grace 1869, every creature should hear the gospel! I believe we have enough Christians here in London to make London hear the gospel. I mean, we have enough converted men and women, if all bestirred themselves, to make London ring from end to end, as once did Nineveh. One man awoke Nineveh with his monotonous cry, "Yet forty days and Nineveh shall be destroyed." Surely the thousands might yet be as firebrands in the midst of corn if we were but in earnest about this great command. *Deus vult*, believer. God demands this of you; is not this enough?

But, if we seek arguments, let us remember that the preaching of the gospel is everywhere a delight to God. Papists tell us that the offering up of what they call a "sacrament" is an acceptable oblation to God. They miss their mark. The preaching of Christ—that is the true oblation. God smells a sweet savor wherever the name of Jesus is rightly proclaimed. Listen to these words: "We are unto God a sweet saviour of Christ, in them that are saved, and in them that perish."[7] Wherever Christ is preached, God is glad. He is honored; Christ is honored. Even if no result should come (impossible supposition!), yet still the mere preaching of Christ is like the smell of evening incense that goes up unto God, and he accepts it.

Moreover, remember that you are bidden to preach to every creature, each of you as far as you can, because it is by this means that the elect are to be

---

7. 2 Corinthians 2:15.

gathered out from among the sons of men. You know not who they are, therefore tell of Christ to everyone. You know not who will accept it; you know not whose heart will be broken by the divine hammer. It is yours to try the hammer of truth on the hard heart. You are not the discoverer of God's chosen, but the gospel is, and as the gospel is preached it will attract to itself, by its own power, through the Holy Spirit, such as God has ordained unto eternal life.

Brothers and sisters, I do pray you preach the gospel of Jesus Christ for your own sakes, if there were no other reason. Depend upon it, your own spiritual vigor will be very much enhanced by your labors of love and your zeal for the service of Christ. I have remarked it as an invariable thermometer by which to gauge the spirituality of a man's heart. Whether he is either doing or not doing something for Christ will tell upon his life and conversation. The tree is not only known by its fruit, as to what kind of tree it is, but also as to what its degree of life is. "If you keep his commandments and bring forth much fruit, you are disciples indeed," but if there be only a little fruit shriveled there on the topmost bough, scarce worth the gathering, why then you are his disciples, but you can scarcely say that you are his disciples indeed.

Did you ever feel the joy of winning a soul for Christ? If so, you will need no better argument for attempting to spread the knowledge of his name among every creature. I tell you, there is no joy out of heaven that excels it—the grasp of the hand of one who says, "By your means I was turned from darkness to light, rescued from drunkenness, or reclaimed perhaps from the grossest vices to love and serve my Savior." To see your spiritual children around you and to say, "Here am I, and these whom you have given me." Oh! The trials and griefs of life sit lightly upon a heart where the triumphs of grace are present. A man might well endure to stand and preach upon a burning bundle of sticks if he could be sure that the burning of his body would secure the salvation of his congregation. Do, for your own happiness's sake, seek to teach to others what the Lord has first taught to you.

I might multiply these reasons, but it will, perhaps, be best to come back to the first one of all— your Master wills it, and therefore preach his gospel to every creature. The day is coming when his gospel shall be known throughout the world. Many things have hindered it. Nights of darkness, years of oppression have lasted long, and the minds of men have been sitting in the valley of the shadow of death. But, as surely as God is God, better days are coming.

"The light that shines from Zion's hill" shall gild the top of every mountain. Every land shall yet behold the feet of them who bring glad tidings and that publish salvation. In spite of the prophecies of certain men in these days, I still cling to the old faith of the church that there shall be a universal triumph of our holy faith before yet the world is given up to the dissolving element. The gods of the heathen shall be shaken from their pedestals. The dispensation shall not end till those things that men have worshiped shall be thrown to the moles and the bats. God will yet drag the harlot of the seven hills from her bloodstained throne and make the kings of the earth burn her as with fire.

The day of the vengeance of our God for martyrs' blood shall yet come, and Christ will not end this conflict till he has brought down the two-edged sword upon the very head of his adversary and has laid him prone in the dust. Have patience, sirs, have patience! Things are progressing well enough just now. Our hearts may well be encouraged. We have seen what God's right hand has done for freedom in this our land. Even now the great pulse of time beats heartily and soundly, and by God's good grace and his gracious overruling providence it shall by-and-by be seen that "The day of freedom dawns at length, The Lord's appointed day."

But if it is ever to come, according to the past, it must come through the efforts of God's children, for he ever works by means, and will do so still. Up, you servants of God, and do your duty diligently, perseveringly, continuing to preach the gospel to every creature, for you are workers together with God. You are God's husbandry, his friends and fellow-helpers. Oh! If you would wish to share the joy of those brighter ages, if you would with blissful eye look down the vista of time and foresee the swords beaten into ploughshares, all prescient of the day when the oppressors' thrones shall crumble in the dust—you cannot look with hopeful eye, with a strong nerve on all this unless you stretch forth your hand and say, "I will have a share in that; I will have a share in it today. I will put my little ounce of power into the church. I will throw my little drachm of might into her mission and seek to tell to every creature of the gospel of Jesus Christ."

The Powers We Have to Work with and How We Can Do the Work

But now, closing up this address, we have our work before us and our God to help us, and we accept the challenge. Brothers and sisters, I call you together just as a master workman when he has a work to do calls together his comrades and says, "Now, this is what we have to do. What power have we to work with, and how can we do it?

Those of us who are specially called to preach the gospel must take our part and go on preaching it with all our might. Oh! It is blessed employment, and angels might well envy us that we have such an office committed to us as to preach the gospel. But, brothers, you must not lay all the labor or all the responsibility on one man. A one-man ministry is, indeed, a curse to any church, if that be the only ministry of the church. All ministries must be used.

But all have not the ability to preach. We have some who can teach the young. Are all who can teach the young engaged in that work? Any night there are schools all around here where there will be twice as many children as the teachers present can instruct. It is not so with any institution of ours, but there are dozens of schools around that are inefficient simply for want of teachers. Our people are always engaged in their schools. I have always said, "Never mind what sect it is; if you can, go and teach there." But I must say that over again, for I do not like to see these schools standing still for want of teachers. It is a very happy thing to hear a sermon, but if you can teach children, it is not your duty to prefer your pleasure to your class.

Could not some of you do good in your own houses? Cottage meetings, parlor meetings, drawing room meetings—these are all means of usefulness. Have you tried them? "How many loaves have you?" so said my Master. I want to count the loaves and tell my Master, and I am of opinion that there are some loaves never brought out of the baker's basket yet, some opportunities that have never yet been put to his service. Search and see.

How much good could some of you do by writing letters to others concerning Christ? How many of you might do good by circulating the printed word—Bibles, gospel tracts, and such sermons as will be most likely to profit certain people if they read them? To some of you, it may be, there is committed the talent of money. If you have not the golden tongue, be thankful that you have the golden purse. Speak with that. You are as much bound to speak with that as others with the golden mouth. Whatever gift you may have, put it out at interest, like a good steward, for your Master. Some of you may not be able to speak or to give, but let your holiness and every power you have, according to your ability and opportunity, contribute to the great result of the gospel being preached to every creature.

My joy and crown, my hope and my delight before God, are you in the Lord when I can perceive an earnest heart in you, O you, the people of ray charge. There are some here of whom I am not ashamed to speak, whose piety is apostolic, whose generosity and zeal are like those of the early church. But there are others of whom we may well speak with hesitation, for if they be consecrated to Christ at all, the consecration seems to have taken but small effect. They are diligent enough in business, but as for fervency of spirit, where is that? In what respects can they be said to serve the Lord? Let each one begin to question himself, "What have I done to carry out the Master's command?" And if you make up a sorrowful total, do not sit down and waste the time in vain regrets, but be humbled and pray God that no man's blood may be laid at your door.

I do urge you—oh! how I would do it if my tongue had language such as I desire to possess! But let me urge you, every one of you, in the future to be putting out the fullness of your strength for him whose bloody sweat, cross, and passion have made you debtors to him for your very lives. By him who died on yonder tree accursed for you, by him who went away to prepare a place for you and who stands pleading still at God's right hand with never-ceasing zeal for you, I come in his name and at his command to entreat, to exhort you to spend and be spent to glorify his name among the sons of men. Search out and look what you can do, and whatsoever your hand finds to do, do with all your might, for the grave will soon open for you, and there is no work nor device in the grave whither you are hastening.

"Up, guards, and at them!" was said in the day of battle, and I may still say it to every Christian. In these days, when popery gathers her might and infidelity shoots forth her poisoned arrows, let none of us be wanting in the day of battle, lest the angels should say, as said the angel of the Lord, "Curse you, Meroz, curse you bitterly the inhabitants thereof because they came not to the help of the Lord, to the help of the Lord against the mighty."

The best thing to do for truth and righteousness is to promote personal piety, and it will bring forth the outgrowth of personal effort. We shall not bless the world by big schemes, mighty theories, gigantic plans. Little by little grows the coral reef on which afterwards gardens are to be planted. Little by little must the kingdom come, each man bringing his mite and laying it down at Jesus's feet. So breaks the light. Beam by beam it comes. One by one come the arrows from the bow of the sun, and at last darkness flies. So must break the everlasting morn. But let us be glad. If the work be slow, it is sure. God will see the work accomplished, and when the morning comes the night shall not succeed it, but it shall scatter the darkness forever. The sun of righteousness goes no more down. The day of the world's morning shall not tarry. The time of her halcyon days shall come, when the light of the sun shall be as the light of seven days and the Lord God shall dwell among men and manifest his glory to the sons of men.

This last moment shall be just used for us to say that there are some here whom we cannot tell to go

and preach the gospel, for they do not know it themselves, and unto the wicked God says, "What have you
to do to declare my statutes?" To such we say, Incline
your ear and listen. Jesus Christ has suffered that sinners might not suffer. He was God's Son. He took the
sins of believers. He was punished in their stead, and
if you will trust him you shall be saved. Trust him, sinner, trust him. May the Holy Spirit persuade you and
give you faith, and unto the Lord Jesus shall be the
glory for ever and ever. Amen.

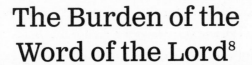

The Burden of the
Word of the Lord[8]

"The burden of the word of the Lord."
(Malachi 1:1)

The prophets of old were no triflers. They did not run about as idle tellers of tales, but they carried a burden. Those who at this time speak in the name of the Lord, if they are indeed sent of God, dare not sport with their ministry or play with their message. They have a burden to bear—"The burden of

---

8. Published in *Metropolitan Tabernacle Pulpit*, Vol. 35 in 1889 by Charles Spurgeon. This is sermon 2114, delivered in 1889, exact date unknown.

the word of the LORD."[9] And this burden puts it out of their power to indulge in levity of life.

I am often astounded at the way in which some who profess to be the servants of God make light of their work. They jest about their sermons as if they were so many comedies or farces. I read of one who said, "I got on very well for a year or two in my pulpit, for my great uncle had left me a large store of manuscripts, which I read to my congregation." The Lord have mercy on his guilty soul! Did the Lord send him a sacred call to bring to light his uncle's moldy manuscripts? Something less than a divine call might have achieved that purpose. Another is able to get on well with his preaching because he pays so much a quarter to a bookseller and is regularly supplied with manuscript sermons. They cost more or less according to the space within which they will not be sold to another clerical cripple.

I have seen the things and have felt sick at the sorry spectacle. What must God think of such prophets as these? In the old times, those whom God sent did not borrow their messages. They had their message directly from God himself, and that message was weighty—so weighty that they called it "the burden of the LORD." He that does not find his ministry a

---

9. Malachi 1:1.

burden now will find it a burden hereafter, which will sink him lower than the lowest hell. A ministry that never burdens the heart and the conscience in this life will be like a millstone about a man's neck in the world to come.

The servants of God mean business; they do not play at preaching, but they plead with men. They do not talk for talking's sake, but they persuade for Jesus's sake. They are not sent into the world to tickle men's ears, nor to make a display of elocution, nor to quote poetry. Theirs is an errand of life or death to souls immortal. They have a something to say that so presses upon them that they must say it. "Woe is unto me if I preach not the gospel!" They burn with an inward fire, and the flame must have vent, for the Word of the Lord is as fire in their bones, consuming them. The truth presses them into its service, and they cannot escape from it. If indeed they be the servants of God, they must speak the things they have seen and heard. The servants of God have no feathers in their caps, but burdens on their hearts.

Furthermore, the true servants of God have something to carry, something worth carrying. There is solid truth, precious truth in their message. It is not froth and foam, phrases and verbiage, stories and pretty things, poetry and oratory, and all that. But there is weight in it of matters that concern heaven and hell, time and eternity. If ever there were men in this world who ought to speak in earnest, they are the men. Those who speak for God must not speak lightly. If there is nothing in what a man has to say, then God never commissioned him, for God is no trifler. If there is no importance in their message—yea, if their message be not of the first and last importance—why do they profess to speak in the name of God? It is constructive blasphemy to impose upon God with our nonsense. The true servant of God has no light weight to bear; he has eternal realities heaped upon him. He does not run merrily as one that has a featherweight to carry, but he treads firmly and often slowly as he moves beneath "the burden of the word of the Lord."[10]

Yet, do not let me be misunderstood at the beginning. God's true servants, who are burdened with his word, right willingly and cheerfully carry that burden. We would not be without it for all the world. Sometimes, do you know, we get tempted, when things do not go right, to run away from it? But we view it as a temptation not to be tolerated for an hour. When some of you do not behave yourselves, and matters in our church get a little out of order, I say to myself, "I wish I could give this up and turn to an

---

10. Malachi 1:1.

employment less responsible and less wearing to the heart." But then I think of Jonah and what happened to him when he ran away to Tarshish, and I remember that whales are scarcer now than they were then, and I do not feel inclined to run that risk.

I stick to my business and keep to the message of my God, for one might not be brought to land quite so safely as the runaway prophet was. Indeed, I could not cease to preach the glad tidings unless I ceased to breathe. God's servants would do nothing else but bear this burden, even if they were allowed to make a change. I had sooner be a preacher of the gospel than a possessor of the Indies. Remember how William Carey, speaking of one of his sons, says, "Poor Felix is shriveled from a missionary to an ambassador." He was a missionary once, and he was employed by the government as an ambassador. His father thought it no promotion but said, "Felix has shriveled into an ambassador." It would be a descent indeed from bearing the burden of the Lord if one were to be transformed into a member of Parliament, a prime minister, a king. We bear a burden, but we should be sorry indeed not to bear it.

The burden the true preacher of God bears is for God, and Christ's behalf, and for the good of men. He has a natural instinct that makes him care for the souls of others, and his anxiety is that none should perish but that all should find salvation through Jesus Christ. Like the Christ who longed to save, so does the true Malachi—messenger of God—go forth with this as his happy, joyful, cheerfully borne burden, that men may turn unto God and live. Yet, it is a burden, for all that. And of that I am going to speak to you. Much practical truth will come before us while we speak of "the burden of the word of the LORD." Pray that the Holy Spirit may bless the meditation to our hearts.

Because It Is the Word of the Lord

And why is the word of the Lord a burden to him who speaks it? Well, first, it is a burden because it is the word of the Lord. If what we preach is only of man, we may preach as we like, and there is no burden about it. But if this Book be inspired—if Yahweh be the only God, if Jesus Christ be God incarnate, if there be no salvation save through his precious blood—then there is a great solemnity about that which a minister of Christ is called upon to preach. It hence becomes a weighty matter with him. Modern thought is a trifle light as air, but ancient truth is weightier than gold.

And, first, the word of the Lord becomes a burden in its reception. I do not think that any man can ever preach the gospel aright until he has had it borne into his own soul with overwhelming energy. You cannot preach conviction of sin unless you have suffered it. You cannot preach repentance unless you have practiced it. You cannot preach faith unless you have exercised it. You may talk about these things, but there will be no power in the talk unless what is said has been experimentally proved in your own soul. It is easy to tell when a man speaks what he has made his own or when he deals in secondhand experience. "Son of man, eat this scroll"; you must eat it before you can hand it out to others.

True preaching is Artesian: it wells up from the great depths of the soul. If Christ has not made a well within us, there will be no outflow from us. We are not proper agents for conveying truth to others if grace has not conveyed it to us. When we get God's word in our studies, we feel it to be a load that bows us to the ground. We are, at times, obliged to get up and walk to and fro beneath the terror of the threatening of God's word, and often are we forced to bow our knee before the glory of some wonderful word of the Lord that beams with excessive grace. We say to ourselves, "These are wonderful truths; how they press upon our hearts!" They create great storms within us; they seem to tear us to pieces. The strong wind of the mighty Spirit blows through the messenger of God, and he himself is swayed to and fro in it as the trees of the forest in the tempest. Hence, even in the reception of the message of God, it is a burden.

The Word of God is a burden in its delivery. Do you think it an easy thing to stand before the people and deliver a message you believe you have received from God? If you so imagine, I wish you would try it. He who finds it easy work to preach will find it hard work to give an account of his preaching at the last great day. One has carefully to look around and think while he is preaching, "I must mind that I do not put this truth in such a way as to exaggerate it into a false-hood. I must not so encourage the weak that I dwarf the strong, nor so commend the strong as to grieve the weak. I must not so preach the grace of God as to give latitude to sin; I must not so denounce sin as to drive men to despair." Our path is often narrow as a razor's edge, and we keep on crying in our spirit, while we are speaking, "Lord, direct me! Lord, help me to deal wisely for you with all these souls!"

The anxieties we feel in connection with our pul-pit work are enough to make us old before our time. I have heard of one who thought he would give up his ministry because he had so small a chapel, into which he could not get more than two hundred people. But a good old man said to him, "You will find it quite hard enough to give a good account of two hundred at the last great day." It is an idle ambition to desire a large congregation, unless that desire is altogether for God's glory, for we only increase our responsibilities when we increase the area of our influence. Still, some are responsible for not having a large congregation. If their dullness keeps people from hearing, they do not thereby escape from responsibility. To speak aright God's Word beneath the divine influence is, in the speaking as well as in the getting of the message, the burden of the Lord.

When we have preached, the gospel becomes a burden in after consideration. "Well, now, it is all done," says one. Is it? Is it all done? You, dear teacher, when you have taught your class today, have you done with your children? You have thought of them upon the Sabbath; will there be no care for them all the week? If your soul is towards your children or your congregation as it ought to be, you will bear them always on your heart. They will never be far away from you. The mother is gone from home. She is out today seeing her sister. Surely she is not caring about her babe, is she? *Is she not?* Why, wherever she is, the tender mother, if she does not bear her child outside her bosom, bears the child inside her heart; her babe is always in her mind. "Can a woman forget her sucking child?" Can a soul winner forget his charge? If God sends any of us to do good to our fellow men and to speak in his name, the souls of men will be a perpetual burden to us, and we shall constantly cry for their salvation and perpetually, with entreaties and tears, go to God for them, and ask him to bless the message we have delivered.

Oh, that we may have in all pulpits ministers who bear the burden of the Lord in the study, in the pulpit, and when the discourse is finished! Once truly a minister, you are always a minister; your burden clings to you. May you, my brothers and sisters, partakers in the holy service of our Lord Jesus Christ, each of you in your measure bear the burden of the word of the Lord, and that continually.

Because of What It Is

I pass to a second point. It is not only a burden because it is so solemnly the word of the Lord and therefore weighty and overwhelming, but next, because of what it is. What is it that the true servant of God has to bear and to preach?

Well, first, it is the rebuke of sin. I have heard of hirelings who preach but never think of rebuking sin. It is with them like as in the story of the old Black preacher, a very popular preacher indeed among his brothers. His master said, "I am afraid some of your people steal chickens, for I am always losing mine. I wish you would next Sunday give them a word about it." "Master," said the preacher, "it would throw such a damp over the congregation if I were to say anything about stealing chickens." So the Black preacher avoided that subject. It seems to me that stealing chickens was the very thing that he ought to have preached about if that was the sin his brothers were guilty of. If a man bears the burden of the word of the Lord, he speaks most to his people upon the evil of which they are most guilty.

Somebody once said to me, "Sir, you were very personal."

I answered, "Sir, I tried to be. Do not think that I am going to apologize for it. If I knew anything that would come home to your heart and conscience concerning sin, I would be sure to say that—just that very thing."

"And what if I should be offended?"

"Well, I should be very sorry that you refused reproof and should feel all the more sure that it was my duty to be very faithful with you. If after much love and prayer you refused the word, I could do no more. But I certainly should not speak with bated breath to please you, and you would despise me if I did."

I remember one in Oliver Cromwell's day who complained to a preacher. He said, "The squire of the parish is very much offended by some remarks you made last Sabbath day about profane swearing."

"Well," said the Puritan preacher, "is the squire in the habit of swearing?"

It was admitted that he was and that he therefore thought himself pointed out by the minister. The Puritan replied to the complaining tenant, "If your lord offends my Lord, I shall not fail to rebuke him for it, and if he is offended, let him be offended." So must every true preacher be careless of man's esteem and speak faithfully; but this is a burden to one of a tender spirit. If there is any topic upon which we must of necessity dwell, it must be upon that sin that is most grieving to the Lord, for we must by no means leave an erring brother unwarned. This is not a work to be coveted. It is neither pleasant to the hearer, nor pleasant to the speaker, and yet to rebuke sin, and to rebuke it sharply, is part of the work of him whom God sends; and this makes the word of the Lord his burden.

And next, the word of the Lord gives a rebuff to human pride. The doctrines of the gospel seem shaped on purpose, among other objects, to bring into contempt all human glory. Here is a man who is morally of a fine and noble nature, but we tell him that he is born in sin and shaped in iniquity; this is a stern duty. Here is a man of a grand righteous character in his own opinion, and we tell him that his righteousness is filthy rags; he will not smile on us for this. Here is a man who can go to heaven by his own efforts, so he thinks, and we tell him that he can do nothing of the sort—that he is dead in trespasses and sins; this will bring us no honor from him. He hopes that, by strong resolves, he may change his own nature and make himself all that God would have him, but we tell him that his resolutions are so much empty wind and will end in nothing; this is likely to earn us his hate.

Behold, the axe is laid at the root of the tree. Man stands a convicted criminal, and if saved must owe his salvation entirely to the gratuitous mercy of God. Condemned and ruined, if he ever escapes from his ruin it must be through the work of the Spirit of God in him and not by his own works. Thus, you see, human nature does not like our message. How it writhes in wrath, how it grinds its teeth against the doctrine that humbles man, crucifies his pride, and nails his glory to the gibbet! Hence, such preaching becomes the burden of the Lord.

And then the true preacher has to come into contact with the vanity of human intellect. We ask of man, "Can you by searching find out God?" You say, "I know." What do you know, poor blind worm? You say, "I am a judge, and I can discern." What can you discern, you who are in the dark and alienated from God by your wicked works? The things of God are hidden from the wise and prudent but revealed unto babes, and the wise and prudent are indignant at this act revealed of divine sovereignty.

"Well," says one, "I quarrel with the Bible." Do you? The only real argument against the Bible is an unholy life. When a man argues against the Word of God, follow him home and see if you cannot discover the reason of his enmity to the word of the Lord. It lies in some form of sin. He whom God sends cares nothing at all about human wisdom, so as to fawn upon it and flatter it, for he knows that "the world by wisdom knew not God" and that human wisdom is only another name for human folly. All the savants and the philosophers are simply those who make themselves to be wise but are not so. Yet to face false science with "the foolishness of preaching" and to set up the cross in the teeth of learned self-sufficiency is a burden from the Lord.

The most heavy burden of the word of the Lord, however, is that which concerns the future. If you be sent of God, and if you preach what God has revealed in his Word, then you say, "He who believes not shall be damned," and you do not hesitate to say that the wrath of God abides on the rejectors of the Savior. you do not hesitate to say—

> There is a dreadful hell
> And everlasting pains,

Where sinners must with devils dwell
In darkness, fire, and chains.

All the romance of the age runs against this.
Everybody says, "Be quiet about the wrath to come,
or you will have everybody down upon you." Be down
upon me then! I will not soften God's Word to please
anybody, and the word of the Lord is very clear on
this matter. If you receive not the Lord Jesus Christ,
you will die in your sins. If you believe not in him, you
must perish from his presence. There is a day coming
when you will die; after this comes another day when
you must appear before the judgment seat of Christ,
and all your actions shall be published, and you shall
be judged for the things done in the body, whether
they be good or be evil, and then you shall receive
the sentence of, "Come, you blessed," or, "Depart, you
cursed."

Do you think we like to preach this? Do you think
that it is any pleasure to the servant of God to deliver
these heavy tidings? Oh, no! We speak in the bitterness of our spirit very often, but we speak because we
dare not refrain. It is infinitely better that men should
be told the truth than that they should be flattered
by a lie into eternal ruin. He ought to have the com-
mendation of all men, not who makes things pleasant
but who speaks things truly. Somebody is preaching

of how to get people out of hell. I preach about how to keep them out of hell. Don't go there. Keep you clear of the fire that never can be quenched. Escape for your lives. Look not behind you; stay not in all the plain but haste to Christ, the mountain of salvation, and put your trust in him. This is the burden of the word of the Lord. We have grief of heart because of the dreadful future men prepare for themselves, namely, "everlasting punishment." We are heavy at heart for the many who will not turn to God but persist in destroying their own souls forever. Oh, why will they die? The prospect of their future is a present misery to us.

Because of the Consequences of Bearing It to You

Now, dear friends, I have in the third place to say that it is a burden not only because it is the word of the Lord and because of what it is, but because of the consequences of our bearing it to you.

Suppose that we do not preach the gospel and warn the wicked man so that he turn not from his iniquity. What then? Hear this voice: "He shall perish, but his blood will I require at your hand." What will my Lord say to me if I am unfaithful to you? "Where is the blood of those people who gathered at

Newington Butts? Where is the blood of that crowd that came together to hear you speak and you did not preach the gospel to them?" Oh, it were better for me that I had never been born than that I should not preach the gospel! "Woe is unto me if I preach not the gospel" of Christ, for men perish where there is not the Word of God!

I remember Mr. Knill's portrait that was once in *The Evangelical Magazine*, that it had written at the bottom of it, "Brothers, the heathen are perishing; will you let them perish?" So is it with men that hear not the glad tidings; they die in sin. Worse still, men are perishing in this country; in the blaze of the light they sit in darkness. Oh, that we might go and find them and tell them of the gospel! For if we carry it not to them, "How shall they believe in him of whom they have not heard? And how shall they hear without a preacher? And how shall they preach except they be sent?"

What makes it more of a burden to me is that men may die if they do hear the word of salvation; men may go from these pews quick into perdition. Those eyes that look on me tonight, oh, how intently and earnestly! O sirs, if you do not look to Christ, you will be lost, however well you may have attended to me. Now, you listen to each word I utter, but I pray you listen to the Word of God, the heavenly Father, who bids you repent and believe in his dear Son, for "except you repent, you shall all likewise perish." So said the Savior. And this, I say, makes the burden of the message, lest some of you should not receive it. I cannot bear that one of you should die unforgiven. I look along these pews, and I remember some of you a good many years ago. You were then in a hopeful state, but you have not received Christ yet. Most faithful hearers you have been, but you have not been doers of the Word. Do not think that I charge you too severely. Have you repented and believed? If not, woe is me that I should bear to you a message that will be a savor of death unto death unto you because you refuse it. For how shall we escape if we neglect so great a salvation? When it has been freely proclaimed to us year after year, what will become of us if we reject it? Do not still refuse to come to Jesus. Do not make me a messenger of death to you. I implore you, receive the message of mercy and be saved.

And, then, it becomes a great burden to me to preach the gospel when I think of what those lose who will not have it. That heaven above—what tongue can describe it? What painter can ever picture it—the heaven above where all is love, joy, peace, and everlasting blessedness? What if you should be shut out? What if against you the door should be closed? There is no opening that door again, remember. Even though you stand and cry, "Lord, Lord!" yet will he not open it to you. May no one of us miss eternal felicity! May no one among us fall into eternal misery!

But here lies the burden of the Lord—in the consequences of our ministry. I recollect walking out to preach nigh unto forty years ago, just when I began my witnessing for the Lord Jesus. As I trudged along with a somewhat older brother who was going to preach at another village station, our talk was about our work, and he said to me, "Does it not strike you as a very solemn thing that we two local preachers are going to do the Lord's work, and much may depend even upon the very hymns we give out and the way we read them?" I thought of that, and I prayed—and often do pray—that I may have the right hymn and the right chapter as well as the right sermon.

Well do I remember a great sinner coming into Exeter Hall, and I read the hymn beginning, "Jesus, lover of my soul," and that first line pierced him in the heart. He said to himself, "Does Jesus love my soul?" He wept because he had not loved the Savior in return, and he was brought to the Savior's feet just by that one line of a hymn. It does make it the burden of the Lord when you see life, death, hell, and worlds to come hanging, as it were, upon the breath of a mortal man by whom God speaks to the souls of his fellows.

This is serious burden bearing. At least, I find it more and more so the longer I am engaged in it.

Because of How People Treat the Word of God

But I pass on to notice one thing more now. It is often the burden of the Lord because of how men treat the Word of God. Upon this I will be very brief. Some trifle with it. I was reading last night an account of how people are said to behave who go to church. It was written by a canon. I daresay he knows. Certainly, some people who go to Nonconformist places are as bad. A servant was asked by her mistress about the sermon. She said it was a very good sermon.

"Where was the text, Martha?"

"Somewhere in the Bible, ma'am."

"What was it about?" She did not recollect a word of it. One question after another is put to her. She tells her mistress that it was a very nice sermon, but she really does not know what it was all about. And the writer goes on to say that a large proportion of our people go off at a tangent while we are talking and their minds are thinking about something else. I hope that it is not quite true of you tonight.

A man once went to hear Mr. Whitefield. He was a shipbuilder, and he said, "Oh, that man! I never

heard such a preacher as that before. When I have
been to other places, I have built a ship from stem to
stern—laid the keel, put the mast in, and finished it
all up while the parson has been preaching. But this
time I was not able to lay a timber. He took me right
away." This preoccupation of human minds makes it
such a burden when we are in earnest to reach the
heart and win the soul. Our people are sitting here in
body, but they are far away in spirit. Yonder sits a good
woman who is meditating as to how she shall leave
her home tomorrow, long enough to get to the shop
to buy those clothes for the children, ready for the
spring weather. A gentleman here tonight wonders
where he has left that diamond ring he took off when
he washed his hands. Do not let that bother you any-
more. Sell the stone and give the money away so that
it will never trouble you again. All sorts of cares come
buzzing around your brains when I am wanting them
to be quite clear to consider holy subjects. Little petti-
fogging cares intrude, and the preacher may speak his
very soul out, but it all goes for nothing. This makes
our work the burden of the Lord.

Then there is another. It is the number of those
who do hear with considerable attention, but they
forget all that they hear. The sermon is all done with
when they have done hearing it. The last drop of dew
is dried up when they get home. Nothing remains of

that which cost the preacher so much thought and prayer. And is it not a hard thing to go on "pegging away and pegging away" and have done nothing? The preoccupied mind is a slate we write on, and then a sponge goes over it all and we have to write each word all over again. Few would choose to roll the stone of Sisyphus, which always fell backward as fast as he laboriously heaved it up the hillside. We are willing to do even this for our Lord, but we are compelled to admit that it is burdensome toil. Poor, poor work with some of you. Ah! It is the burden of the Lord to deal with your souls.

Alas! There are some others who hear to ridicule. They pick out some mannerism, mistake, or something eccentric about the speaker's language, and they carry this home and report it as raw material for fun. The preacher is in anguish to save a soul, and they are thinking about how he pronounces a word. Here is a man endeavoring to pluck sinners from the eternal burnings, and these very sinners are all the while thinking about how he moves his legs, how he lifts his hand, or how he pronounces a certain syllable. Oh, it is sickening work—soul-sickening work! It is the "burden of the word of the Lord" when our life-or-death message is received in that way.

But when it is received rightly, then are we in the seventh heaven! Oh, well do I remember one night preaching three sermons, one after the other, and I think I could have preached thirty if time had held out. It was in a Welsh village, where I had gone into the chapel and simply meant to expound the Scripture while another brother preached. He preached in Welsh, and when it was done, the question was put whether Mr. Spurgeon would not preach. I had not come prepared, but I did preach, and there was a melting time, and then we sang a hymn. I think we sang one verse seven or eight times over; the people were all on fire. The sound seemed to make the shingles dance on the top of the chapel. When I had done, we asked those who were impressed to stop. They all stopped, and so I had to preach again; and a second time they all stopped, and I had to preach again. It got on to past eleven o'clock before they went away. Eighty-one came forward and joined the churches afterwards. It was but a few months before the terrible accident at Pisca, and many of those converted that night perished in the pit. God had sent his Spirit on that glorious night to save them, that they might be ready when he should call them home. It was grand work to preach, for they sucked in the word as babes take in the milk. They took it into their hearts; it saved their souls. Would we had many such opportunities, and then the Word of the Lord would be no burden, but like the wings of a bird to make us mount on high, and joy would fill every heart!

Because the Preacher Must Give an Account

And now I must not detain you, but I want to say, in the fifth place, the word of the Lord is the greatest burden to the true teacher's heart because he remembers that he will have to give an account. They are all down, those fifty-two Sabbaths, and those weeknight opportunities, they are all down in the heavenly record, and the writing will be forthcoming when required. There will come a time when it will be said, "Preacher, give an account of your stewardship." And at the same time a voice will be heard, "Hearers, give an account of your stewardship, too." What a mercy it will be if you and I together shall give in our accounts with joy and not with grief! For a mournful account will be unprofitable for you. What sort of sermons shall I wish I had preached when I come to die? What sort of sermons will you wish that you had heard when you lie on your last beds? You will not wish that you had heard mere flimsy talk and clever speeches. Oh, no! You will say as a dying man, "I bless God for weighty words, earnestly spoken, that were a blessing to my soul." I will say no more upon that, although it is the pressing point of the whole matter. Brothers, pray for the preacher. Brothers, pray for yourselves.

I have only these two or three practical words to say. We have to bear the burden of the Lord, but there was one, the Head of our confraternity, the great Lord of all true gospel preachers, who bore a far heavier burden. "He his own self bare our sins in his own body on the tree." Preacher, teacher, do you ever get weary? Look to him as he bows beneath his cross, take up your burden cheerfully, and follow after Jesus.

If this work be a burden, we also rejoice in One who can help us. There is One who can make the burden light or strengthen the shoulder to bear the heavy yoke. Dear people, pray for us that this great Helper may enable us to bear the burden of his Word to your souls. Do not pray that it may not be a burden. Pray that it may be a burden that crushes your pastor to the very dust. God forbid that he should ever preach without its being a load to him! But pray that he may then be sustained under it and for every true preacher of the gospel pray the same prayer. If the Lord be with us, we shall not faint but go from strength to strength.

Since it is a burden in itself, I ask you not to make it any heavier. Do not make it intolerable. Some add to it greatly and wantonly. Who are these? Well, I will tell you: inconsistent professors. When people point to such and such a member of the church, and say,

"That is your Christian!" this makes our burden doubly oppressive. What a spoil it is to our testimony for Christ when outsiders can point to one and another, and say, "That is how those Christians act!" Do not plunge us in this sorrow. I do not know why I should be blamed for all the offenses of everybody that comes to hear me. Can I keep you all right? Are you like chessmen that I can move at pleasure to any square on the board? I cannot be responsible for any one person; how can I be the guardian of all? Yet the preacher of God's truth is held responsible by many for matters over which he has no power, and this injustice makes his burden heavy.

And, next, do not make our burden heavier by your silence. There was a man of God who had been a very distinguished preacher, and when he lay dying he was much troubled in his mind. He had been greatly admired and much followed. He was a fine preacher of the classical sort, and one said to him, "Well, my dear sir, you must look back upon your ministry with great comfort." "Oh, dear!" said he, "I cannot; I cannot. If I knew that even one soul had been led to Christ and eternal life by my preaching I should feel far happier, but I have never heard of one." What a sad, sad thing for a dying preacher! He died, was buried, and there was a goodly company of people at the grave, for he was highly respected, and deservedly so. One who heard him make that statement was standing at the grave, and he noticed a gentleman in mourning, looking into the tomb, and sobbing with deep emotion. He said to him, "Did you know this gentleman who has been buried?"

He replied, "I never spoke to him in my life."

"Then what is it that so affects you?"

He said, "Sir, I owe my eternal salvation to him." He had never told the minister this cheering news, and the good man's deathbed was rendered dark by the silence of a soul that he had blessed. This was not right. A great many more may have found the Lord by his means, but he did not know of them and was therefore in sore trouble. Do tell us when God blesses our word to you. Give all the glory to God, but give us the comfort of it. The Holy Spirit does the work, but if we are the means in his hands, do let us know it, and we will promise not to be proud. It is due to every preacher of Christ that if he has been blessed to the conversion of a soul he should be allowed to see the fruit of his labors. And when he does not see it, it adds very sadly to "the burden of the Word of the LORD."

Do you not think that you add to my burden, too, if you do not aid me in the Lord's work? What a lot of idle Christians we have Christian people who might sing, like mendicants in the street, "And got no work to do, And got no work to do!" What a shameful chorus when the world is dying for lack of true workers! There is a Sunday school; do you know it? "Oh, yes, we know there is one of those excellent institutions" connected with our place of worship. Did you ever visit it? Have you ever helped in it? There is an Evangelists' Society, and young men go out to preach. "Oh, dear!" say you, "I never thought of that." Why do you not go out to preach yourself? Some of you could if you would. What are you at? There are districts where there are tracts to be distributed. Do you know anything about house-to-house visitation? I speak to some who do nothing whatever, unless it be a little grumbling.

I wonder whether we shall ever have a day such as the bees celebrate in its due season. You may, perhaps, have seen them dismissing the unproductives. It is a remarkable sight. They say to themselves, "Here is a lot of drones, eating our honey but never making any; let us turn them out." There is a dreadful buzz, is there not? But out they go. I do not propose either to turn you out or to make a buzz, but if ever those who do work for Christ should burn with a holy indignation against do-nothings, some of you will find the place too hot for you! I am sorrowfully afraid that it will thin my congregation and lessen the number of church members. I have but little to complain of among my people, but still, as there is a lazy corner in every village, there is the same in this community. You increase the burden of those who do work if you are not working with them.

But the greatest increase of the burden comes from those who do not receive the gospel at all. May there not be one such here tonight, but may everyone now look to Jesus and live! I shall close by asking you to sing the gospel. Oh, that you may have it in your hearts! The final closing word is this—

> There is life in a look at the Crucified
>   One;
> There is life at this moment for thee;
> Then look, sinner— look unto him, and
>   be saved—
> Unto him who was nail'd to the tree.

Preaching! Man's Privilege and God's Power[11]

*"For Herod feared John, knowing that
he was a just man and holy, and observed
him; and when he heard him, he did
many things, and heard him gladly."*
(Mark 6:20)

The preaching of the Word has exceeding power.
John commenced his ministry as an obscure
individual, a man who led an almost hermit life. He

---

11. Published in *Metropolitan Tabernacle Pulpit*, Vol. 6 in 1860 by
Charles Spurgeon. This is sermon 347, delivered on November
25, 1860.

begins to preach in the wilderness of Judea, but his cry is so powerful that before he has spoken many days, multitudes wait upon his words. He continues, clothed in that shaggy garment and living on the simplest of food, still to utter the same cry of preparation for the kingdom of heaven—Repent! repent! repent! And now, not only the multitude but the teachers, the respectable part of the community, come to listen to him. The scribes and Pharisees sit down by Jordan's banks to listen to the Baptist's word. So powerful is his preaching that many of all ranks—publicans, sinners, and soldiers—come unto him and are baptized by him in Jordan confessing their sins. Nay, the scribes and Pharisees themselves seek baptism at his hands. Boldly, however, he repulses them, tells them to bring forth fruits of repentance and warns them that their descent from Abraham does not entitle them to the blessings of the coming kingdom of the great Messiah. His word rings from one end of Judea to the other.

All men wonder what this can mean, and already there begins to be a feeling in the hearts of men that Messiah is at hand. Herod himself hears of John, and now you behold the spectacle of a cruel and unrighteous king sitting humbly to listen to this stern reformer. The Baptist changes not his preaching. The same boldness that had made him rebuke the common people and their teachers now leads him to defy the wrath of Herod himself. He touches him in his most tender place, strikes his favorite sin, dashes down his idle lust to the ground, counts it his business not to speak of truth in generals but in particulars. Yea, he tells him to his very face, "It is not lawful for you to take to yourself your brother's wife."

Oh, what a power there is in the Word of God! I do not find that the Pharynx with all their learning had moved Herod. I discover not that the most mighty of the Grecian philosophers, or of the Gnostics who were then in existence, had any power to reach the heart of Herod. But the simple, plain preaching of John, his declaration of the Word with all honesty and simplicity had power to pin Herod by the ear, to vibrate in his heart and to awaken his conscience, for sure we are it was awakened. If the awakening did not end in his conversion, at any rate it made him troubled in his sins so that he could not go on peaceably in iniquity.

Ah, my dear friends, we want nothing in these times for revival in the world but the simple preaching of the gospel. This is the great battering ram that shall dash down the bulwarks of iniquity. This is the great light that shall scatter the darkness. We need not that men should be adopting new schemes and new plans. We are glad of the agencies and assistants that are continually arising, but after all, the true Jerusalem blade, the sword that can cut to the piercing asunder of the joints and marrow, is preaching the Word of God. We must never neglect it, never despise it. The age in which the pulpit it despised will be an age in which gospel truth will cease to be honored. Once put away God's ministers, and you have to a great extent taken the candle out of the candlestick, quenched the lamps that God hath appointed in the sanctuary. Our missionary societies need continually to be reminded of this; they get so busy with translations, so diligently employed with the different operations of civilization, with the founding of stores, with the encouragement of commerce among a people that they seem to neglect—at least in some degree—that which is the great and master weapon of the minister: the foolishness of preaching by which it pleases God to save them that believe.

Preaching the gospel will effectually civilize, while introducing the arts of civilization will sometimes fail. Preaching the gospel will lift up the barbarian, while attempts to do it by philosophy will be found ineffectual. We must go among them and tell them of Christ; we must point them to heaven; we must lead them to the cross should they be elevated in their character and raised in their condition. But by no other means. God forbid that we should begin to depreciate preaching. Let us still honor it; let us look to it as God's ordained instrumentality, and we shall yet see in the world a repetition of great wonders wrought by the preaching in the name of Jesus Christ.

Today I shall want your attention to a subject that concerns us all, but more especially those who, being hearers of the Word, are hearers only and not doers of the same. I shall first attempt to show the blessedness of hearing the Word of God; secondly, the responsibilities of the hearer; and then, thirdly, those accompaniments that are necessary to go with the hearing of the Word of God to make it effectual to save the soul.

The Blessedness of Hearing the Word

First of all, my dear friends, let us speak a little about the blessedness of hearing the Word. The prophet constantly asserts, "Blessed are the ears that hear the things that we hear; and blessed are the eyes that see the things which we see." Prophets and kings desired it long but died without the sight. Often do the seers of old use language similar to this: "Blessed is the people that know the joyful sound, they shall walk, O Lord, in the light of your countenance." Godly men accept it as an omen of happy times when their eyes should see their teachers. The angels sang the blessedness of it when they descended from on high, singing, "Glory to God in the highest, and on earth peace, goodwill toward men. Behold, we bring you good tidings of great joy, which shall be unto you and to all people." The angels' song is in harmony with the seers' testimony. Both conjoin to prove what I assert, that we are blessed in having the privilege of listening to God's Word.

Let us enlarge upon this point. If we reflect upon what the preaching of the Word is, we shall soon see that we are highly privileged in enjoying it. The preaching of the Word is the scattering of the seed. The hearers are the ground on which the good seed falls. Those who hear not the Word are as the arid desert, which has never seen a handful of the good corn; or as the unplowed waves of the sea that have never been gladdened with the prospect of a harvest. But when the sower goes forth to sow seed, he scatters it broadcast upon you who hear, and there is to you the hope that in you the good seed shall take root and bring forth fruit a hundredfold. True, some of you may be but wayside hearers, and evil birds may soon devour the seed. At least, it does fall upon you, nor is it the fault of the seed, but of the ground if that seed does not grow. True, you may be as stony-ground hearers, who for a while receive the Word and rejoice therein, but having no root in yourselves, the seed may wither away. That again, I say, does not diminish your privilege, though it increases your guilt, inasmuch as it is no fault of the seed nor of the sun but the fault of the stony ground if the fruit is not nourished unto perfection. And you, inasmuch as you are the field, the broad acres upon which the gospel husbandman scatters the precious grain, you enjoy the privilege that is denied heathens and idolaters.

Again, the kingdom of heaven is likened unto a net that is cast into the sea and gathers of divers kinds. Now you represent the fish of the sea, and it is happy indeed for you that you are where the net is thrown, for there is at least the hope that you may be entangled in its meshes and may be drawn out of the sea of sin and gathered into the vessels of salvation. If you were far, far away, where the net is never cast, there would be no hope of your being caught therein. But here you are gathered round the fisherman's humble boat, and as he casts his net into the sea, he hopes that some of you may be caught therein—and assuredly gracious is your privilege! But if you be not caught, it shall not be the fault of the net but the fault of your own willfulness, which shall make you fly from it lest you be graciously taken therein.

Moreover, the preaching of the gospel is very much in this day like the mission of Christ upon earth. When Christ was on earth he went about walking through the midst of sick folk, and they laid them in their beds by the wayside so that as Jesus passed by they might touch the hem of his garment and be made whole. You, today, when you hear the Word are like the sick in their beds where Jesus passes by. You are like blind Bartimaeus sitting by the wayside begging in the very road along which the Son of David journeys. Lo, a multitude have come to listen to him. He is present wherever his truth is preached: "Lo, I am with you always, even to the ends of the world."[12] You are not like sick men in their chambers or sick men far away in Tyre and Sidon, but you are like the men who lay at Bethesda's pool under the five porches, waiting for the moving of the water. Angel of God, move the waters this day! or rather, O Jesus, give you grace to the impotent man that he may now step in.

Yet further, we may illustrate the privilege of those who hear the Word by the fact that the Word of God is the bread of heaven. I can only compare this great number of people gathered here today to the sight that was seen upon the mountain in the days of Jesus. They were hungry, and the disciples would have sent them away. But Jesus bade them sit down in ranks upon the grass, as you are sitting down in rows here, and there were but a few barley loaves and five small fishes (fit type and representation of the minister's own poverty

---

12. Matthew 28:20.

of words and thoughts!). But Jesus blessed the bread and the fishes, and broke them, and they were multiplied, and they did all eat and were filled. So you are as these men. God give you grace to eat. There is not given to you a stone instead of bread, nor a scorpion instead of an egg; but Christ Jesus shall be fully and freely preached to you. May you have appetites to long for the Word, faith to partake of the Word, and may it be to you the bread of life sent down from heaven.

Yet often in Scripture we find the Word of God compared to a light. "The people which sat in darkness saw a great light."[13] "Unto them that dwell in darkness, and in the valley of the shadow of death, has a great light arisen." Those who hear not the Word are men that grope their way not only in a fog but in a thick Egyptian darkness that may be felt. Before your eyes today is held up the flaming torch of God's Word to show you your path through the thick darkness. Nay, today there is not only a torch, but in the preaching of the Word the Sun of Righteousness himself arises with healing beneath his wings. You are not they who grope for the wall like blind men; you are not as they who are obliged to say, "We see not the path to heaven; we know not the way to God; we fear we shall never be reconciled to Christ." Behold, the

---

13. Matthew 4:6.

light of heaven shines upon your eyeballs, and if you perish, you must perish willfully; if you sink into hell, it will be with the path to heaven shining before you; if damned, it will be not because you do not know the way of salvation but because you willfully and wickedly put it from you and choose for yourselves the path of death. It must even be then a privilege to listen to the Word, if the Word be as a light, as bread, as healing, as a gospel net, and as divine seed.

Once more let me remind you: There is yet a greater privilege connected with the Word of God than this—for all this were nothing without the last. As I look upon a multitude of unconverted men and women, I am reminded of Ezekiel's vision. He saw lying in the valley of Hinnom multitudes of bones, the flesh of which had been consumed by fire, and the bones themselves were dried as in a furnace, scattered hither and thither. There with other bones in other charnel houses, lying scattered at the mouths of other graves, but Ezekiel was not sent to them; to the valley of Hinnom was he sent, and there alone. And he stood by faith and began to practice the foolishness of preaching: "You dry bones hear the word of the Lord; thus says the Lord, you dry bones live." And as he spoke there was a rustling; each bone sought its fellow. And as he spoke again, these bones united and stood erect; as he continued his discourse the flesh clothed the skeleton. When he concluded by crying, "Come from the winds, and breathe upon these slain, that they may live," they stood upon their feet an exceeding great army.

The preached Word is like Ezekiel's prophecy; life goes forth with the word of the faithful minister. When we say, "Repent!" we know that sinners cannot repent of themselves, but God's grace sweetly constrains them to repent. When we bid them believe, it is not because of any natural capacity for faith that lies within them but because the command "Believe and live," when given by the faithful minister of God, has in it a quickening power, as much as when Peter and John said to the man with the withered hand, "In the name of Jesus of Nazareth, stretch out your hand," and it was done. So do we say to the dead in sin, "Sinner, live; repent and be converted; repent and be baptized every one of you in the name of the Lord Jesus."

Owned of God the Spirit, it becomes a quickening cry, and you are made to live. Blessed are the dry bones that lay in a valley where Ezekiel prophesies; and blessed are you that are found where Jesus Christ's name is preached, where his power is invoked by a heart that believes in its energy, where his truth is preached to you by one who, despite many mistakes, knows this one thing—that Christ is both the power of God and the wisdom of God unto everyone who believes. This consideration alone then—the peculiar power of the Word of God—might compel us to say, "That indeed there is a blessedness in hearing it."

But, my dear friends, let us look at it in another light. Let us appeal to those who have heard the Word and have received good in their own souls by it. Men and brothers, I speak to hundreds of you who know in your own soul what the Word of God is. Let me ask you—you who have been converted from a thousand crimes, you who have been picked from the dung-hill and made to sit among the princely children of God—let me ask you what you think of the preaching of the Word. Why, there are hundreds of you men and women, who if this were the proper time and occasion, would rise from your seat and say, "I bless God that ever I listened to the preached Word. I was a stranger to all truth, but I was enticed to come and listen, and God met with me."

Some of you can look back to the first Sunday on which you ever entered a place of worship for twenty years, and that place was this very hall. Here you came an unaccustomed worshiper to tread God's hallowed floor. You stood and knew not what you were at. You wondered what the service of God's house could be. But you have reason to remember that Sabbath day, and you will have reason to remember it to all eternity. Oh that day! It broke your bonds and set you free; that day aroused your conscience and made you feel your need of Christ. That day was a blessed turning point in your history, in which you were led to escape from hell, turn your back on sin, and fly for refuge to Christ Jesus.

Since that day let me ask you, what has the Word of God been to you? Has it not been constantly a quickening word? You have grown dull and careless during the week; has not the Sabbath sermon stirred you up afresh? You have sometimes all but lost your hope, and has not the hearing of the Word revived you? Why, I know that some of you have come up to the house of God as hungry men would come to a place where bread was distributed; you come to the house of God with a light and happy step, as thirsty men would come to a flowing well, and you rejoice when the day comes round. You only wish there were seven Sabbath days a week, that you might always be listening to God's Word. You can say with Dr. Watts, "Father, my soul would still abide within your temple, near your side. And if my feet must hence depart, still keep your dwelling in my heart."

Personally I have to bless God for many good books. I thank God for Dr. Doddridge's *Rise and Progress of Religion*; I thank God for Baxter's *Call to the Unconverted*; for Alleyne's *Alarm to Sinners*; I bless God for James's *Anxious Enquirer*. But my gratitude

most of all is due to God, not for books but for the
living Word—and that too addressed to me by a poor
uneducated man, a man who had never received any
training for the ministry and probably will never be
heard of in this life, a man engaged in business, no
doubt of a menial kind during the week, but who had
just enough of grace to say on the Sabbath, "Look
unto me and be you saved all you ends of the earth."
The books were good, but the man was better. The
revealed Word awakened me—the living Word saved
me—and I must ever attach peculiar value to the hearing of the truth, for by it I received the joy and peace
in which my soul delights.

But further, my dear hearers, the value of the Word
preached and heard may be estimated by the opinions
the lost have of it now. Hearken to one man, it is not a
dream nor a picture of my imagination I now present
to you, it is one of Jesus Christ's own graphic descrip-
tions. There lies a man in hell who has heard Moses
and the prophets. His time is passed, and he can hear
them no more. But so great is the value he attaches
to the preached Word that he says, "Father Abraham,
send Lazarus, for I have five brothers. Let him tes-
tify unto them, lest they also come into this place of
torment." He felt that if Lazarus could speak—speak
personally his own personal testimony to the truth,
that peradventure they might be saved. Oh! What

would the damned in hell give for a sermon could they but listen once more to the church-going bell and go up to the sanctuary! Ah, my brothers, they would consent, if it were possible, to bear ten thousand years of hell's torments if they might but once more have the Word preached to them!

Ah! If I had a congregation such as that would be, of men who have tasted the wrath of God, of men who know what an awful thing it is to fall into the hands of an angry God. Oh, how would they lean forward to catch every word, with what deep attention would they all regard the preacher, each one saying, "Is there a hope for me? May I not escape from the place of doom? Good God! May this fire not be quenched and I be plucked as a brand from the burning?" Value then, I pray you, the privilege while you have it now. We are always foolish, and we never value mercy till we lose it. But I do adjure you cast not aside this folly, value it while it is called today, value that which once lost will seem to us to be priceless beyond all conception—estimated then at its true worth, invaluable, and precious beyond a miser's dream.

Let me again ask you to value it in a brighter light—by the estimation of the saints before the throne. You glorified ones, what think you of the preaching of the Word? Hark to them! Will they not sing it forth: "Faith came to us by hearing, and hearing by the

Word of God. It was by it that we were led to confess our sins; by it we were led to wash our robes and make them white in the blood of the Lamb"? I am sure they before the throne think not lightly of God's ministers. They would not speak with cold language of the truth of the gospel that is preached in your ears. No, in their eternal hallelujahs they bless the Lord who sent the gospel to them as they sing, "Unto him who loved us and washed us from our sins in his blood, unto him be glory for ever and ever." Value, then, the preaching of the Word, and count yourselves happy that you are allowed to listen to it.

The Responsibilities of the Hearer of the Word

My second head deals more closely with the text, and I hope it will likewise appeal more closely to our consciences: the responsibilities of the hearer of the Word.

Herod, you will perceive, went as far as very many of us, perhaps farther than some, and yet was lost. Our responsibilities concerning the Word do not end with hearing it. Herod heard it, but hearing is not enough. You may sit for fifty years in the sanctuary of God hearing the gospel and be rather the worse than the better for all you have heard if it ends in hearing. It is not the Word entering into one ear and coming forth out of the other ear that converts the soul, but it is the echoing of the Word down in the very heart and the abiding of the truth in the conscience.

I know there are very many who think they have fulfilled all their religion when they go to their church or chapel. Let us not deceive you in this thing. Your churchgoing and your chapel going, though they give you great privileges yet involve the most solemn responsibilities. Instead of being in themselves saving, they may be damning unless you avail yourselves of the privileges presented by them. I doubt not that hell is crammed with church and chapel goers and that there are whole wards in that infernal prison house filled with men who heard the Word but who stopped there, who sat in their pews but never fled to Christ, who listened to the call but did not obey it.

"Yes," says one, "but I do more than simply hear the Word, for I make choice of the most earnest preacher I can find." So did Herod, and yet he perished. He was not a hearer of a man with a soft tongue, for John did not speak as one clothed in fine raiment. John was not a reed shaken with the wind. He was a prophet, "Yea, I say unto you, and more than a prophet." Faithful in all his house as a good servant of his God. There was never a more honest and faithful preacher than John. And you too may with care have selected the most excellent minister, not for his eloquence but for his earnestness; not for his talent but for his power of faith. And you may listen to him, and that too with attention, and after all may be a castaway. The responsibilities involved in listening to such a man may be so weighty that, like a millstone about your neck, they may help to sink you lower than the lowest hell. Take heed to yourselves that you rest not in the outward Word, however fitly spoken or however attentively heard, but reach forward to something deeper and better.

"Yes," says a third, "but I do not only hear the most earnest preacher, but I go out of my way to hear him. I have left my parish church, for instance, and I come walking five or six miles—I am willing to walk ten or even twenty if I can but hear a sermon—and I am not ashamed to mingle with the poor. I may have rank and position in life, but I am not ashamed to listen to the earnest preacher, though he should belong to the most despised of sects" Yea, and Herod did the like. Herod was a king and yet listened to the peasant-prophet. Herod is clothed in purple and yet listens to the Baptist in his shaggy garment. While Herod fared sumptuously every day, he who ate locusts and wild honey reproves him boldly to his face. And with all this, Herod was not saved. So, also, you may walk many a mile to listen to the truth, and that year after year, but unless you go further than that, unless you obey the Word, unless it sinks deep into your inmost soul, you shall perish still—perish under the sound of the Word—the very Word of God becoming a death knell to your soul, dreadfully tolling you down to deep destruction.

But I hear another object. "I, sir, not only take the trouble to hear, but I hear very gladly. I am delighted when I listen. I am not a captious, critical hearer, but I feel a pleasure in listening to God's Word. Is not that a blessed sign? Do you not think that I must be saved if I rejoice to hear that good sound?" No, my friend, no. It is a hopeful sign, but it is a very uncertain one, for is it not written in our text that Herod heard the Word gladly? The smile might be on his face or the tear in his eye while the Baptist denounced sin; there was something in his conscience that made him feel glad that there was one honest man alive, that in a time of enormous corruption there was one fearless soul who dared with unblanched cheek to correct sin in high places. He was like Henry the Eighth, who when Hugh Latimer presented him on New Year's Day with a napkin on which was embroidered the words, "Whoremongers and adulterers God will judge," instead of casting the preacher into prison, he said, "He was glad there was one man who dared to tell him, and he stands up for you and defends you, but he is as bad a man as there is living."

Oh sirs! I am glad you listen to me. I do hope that the hammer may yet break your hearts, but I do conjure you, give up your sins. Oh! For your own soul's sake, do not abide in your transgressions, for I warn you, if I have spoken faithfully to you, you cannot sin so cheaply as other men. I have never prosed away to you. I have never been too polite to warn you of perdition. I speak to you in rough and earnest terms— I may claim that credit without egotism. If you perish, sirs, it will little boot you that you stood up in my defense; it will little serve you that you tried to screen the minister from slander and from calumny. I would have you think of yourselves, even though you thought less of me and my reputation. I would have you love yourselves and so escape from hell and fly to heaven while yet the gate of mercy stands on the jar, and the hour of mercy is not passed for ever. Think not, I say, that hearing the Word gladly is enough; you may do so and yet be lost.

But more than that. "Ah," says one, "you have just anticipated what I was about to say. I not only listen gladly, but I respect the preacher. I would not hear a man say a word against him." It was so with Herod. "He observed John," it is said, "and he accounted him a just man and a holy." And yet though he honored the preacher, he was lost himself. Ah! What multitudes go to our fashionable places of worship, and as they come out they say to one another, "What a noble sermon!" And then they go to their houses and sit down and say, "What a fine turn he gave to that period! What a rich thought that was! What a sparkling metaphor!" And is it for this that we preach to you? Is your applause the breath of our nostrils? Do you think that God's ministers are sent into the world to tickle your ears and be unto you as one who plays a merry tune on a goodly instrument? God knows I would sooner break stones on the road than be a preacher for oratory's sake. I would never stand here to play the hypocrite. No, it is your hearts we want, not your admiration. It is your espousal to Christ and not your love to us. Oh that we could break your hearts and awake your consciences, we would not mind what other results should follow. We should feel that we were accepted of God if we were but felt with power to be God's servants in the hearts and thoughts of men. No, think not that to honor the preacher is enough. You may perish praising the minister in your dying moments.

Yet further, someone may say, "I feel I am a better man through hearing the minister, and is not that a good sign?" Yes, it is a good sign, but it is not a sure one for all that. For Herod they said did many things. Look at the text. It is expressly said there, "He observed him, and when he heard him, he did many things." I should not wonder after that, that Herod became somewhat more merciful in his government, somewhat less exacting, a little more outwardly moral, and though he continued in his lasciviousness, yet he tried to cover it up with respectable excuses. "He did many things." That was doing a very long way, but Herod was Herod still.

And you, sirs, it may be, have been led to give up drunkenness through the preaching of the Word, to shut up the shop that used to be opened on a Sunday. You cannot now swear; you would not now cheat. It is good; it is very good. But it is not enough. All this there may be, but yet the root of the matter may not be in you. To honor the Sabbath outwardly will not save you, unless you enter into the rest that remains for the people of God. Merely to close the shop is not enough. The heart itself must be shut up against the love of sin. To cease blasphemy is not sufficient, though it is good, for there may be blasphemy in the heart when there is none upon the tongue. "Except you be converted and become as little children, you shall in no wise enter the kingdom of heaven." For "Except a man be born again he cannot see the kingdom of God." The Lord grant that you may not rest with outward cleansing, with moral purification, but strike deeper into the root, soul, and marrow of these blessings, the change of your heart, the bringing of your soul into union with Christ.

One thing I must also remark about Herod, with the Greek text in view "He did many things," will allow me to infer that he felt many doubts. As a good old commentator says, "John smote him so hard that he could not help feeling it. He gave him such home blows that he could not but be bruised every now and then, and yet though his conscience was smitten, his heart was never renewed." It is a pleasant sight to see men weep under the Word—to mark them tremble—but then we remember Felix. Felix trembled, but he said, "Go your way for this time; when I have a more convenient season I will send for you." Happy is the minister who hears the people say, "Almost you persuade us to be Christians." But then, we remember Agrippa—we remember how he returns to his sins and seeks not the Savior. We are glad if your consciences are awakened, we rejoice if you are made to doubt and question yourselves, but we mourn because your doubts are so transient, because your goodness is as the morning cloud and as the early dew.

I have tracked some of you to your houses. I have known of some who after a solemn sermon when they got home could scarcely eat their meal. They sit down, leaning their head on their hand. The wife is glad to think that her husband is in a hopeful state. He rises from his seat; he goes up stairs; he walks about the house he says he is miserable. At last he comes down and sets his teeth together and says "Well, if I am to be damned I shall be damned; if I am to be saved I shall be saved, and there's an end of it." Then he rouses himself, saying, "I cannot go to hear that man again; he is too hard with me. I must either give up my sins or give up listening to the Word; the two things will not exist together." Happy, I say, are we to see that man troubled, but our unhappiness is so much the greater when we see him shaking it off—the dog returning to his vomit and the sow that was washed to her wallowing in the mire. O God, save us from this, let us never be men who spring up fairly but wither away suddenly and disappoint all hope. O God, let us not be as Balaam, who prayed that his last end might be with the righteous but returned to defy Israel, to provoke the Lord God, and to perish in the midst of his iniquity.

And now I hear many of you say, "Well if all these things are not enough, what is it that is expected of the hearer of the Word?" Spirit of God! Help us so to speak that the Word may come home to all! Believer in Christ, if you would hear the Word to profit, you must hear it obediently. You must hear it as James and John did when the Master said, "Follow me," and they left their nets and their boats and then followed him.

You must do the Word as well as hear it, yielding up your hearts to its sway, being willing to walk in the road it maps, to follow the path it lays before you.

Hearing it obediently, you must also hear it personally, not for others but for yourselves alone. You must be as Zacchaeus, who was in the sycamore tree and the Master said, "Zacchaeus, make haste and come down, today I must abide in your house."[14] The Word will never bless you till it comes home directly to yourself. You must be as Mary, who when the Master spoke to her, she did not know his voice till he said unto her, "Mary!" and she said, "Rabboni." There must be an individual hearing of the truth and a reception of it for yourself in your own heart.

Then, too, you must hear the truth penitently. You must be as that Mary, who when she listened to the Word must needs go and wash the feet of Jesus with her tears and wipe them with the hairs of her head. There must be tears for your many sins, a true confession of your guilt before God.

But above all you must hear it believingly. The Word must not be unto you as mere sound but as matter of fact. You must be as Lydia, whose heart the Lord opened, or as the trembling jailer, who believed on the Lord Jesus with all his house and was baptized

---

14. Luke 19:5.

forthwith. You must be as the thief who could pray, "Lord, remember me," and who could believe the precious promise given, "Today shall you be with me in Paradise." God give us grace so to listen, and then shall our responsibilities under the Word be cleared up, receiving the power of the Word into our conscience with demonstration of the Holy Spirit and fruits agreeable to our profession.

The Needful Accompaniments of Hearing the Word

Now to conclude. I want your serious attention to the needful accompaniments of hearing the Word. There are many men who get blessed by the Word through God's sovereign grace without any of the accompaniments of which I am now about to speak. We have connected with us, as a church, a brother in Christ who came into this place of worship with his gin bottle in his pocket one night. A chance hit of mine—as some would have thought it—when I pointed to the man and told him of it, not knowing aught but that the feeling that I was moved thereunto was the man's first awakening. That man came without any preparation, and God blessed the word. Numerous have been the instances, which those who have not proved them deem utterly incredible, in which persons have absolutely come to me after a sermon and begged me not to tell anybody about them, being firmly persuaded from what I said that I knew their private history, whereas I knew no more about them than a stranger in the market. But the Word of God will find men out. Preach the gospel, and it will always find the man out and tell him all his secrets, carrying the lamp of the Lord into the hidden recesses of the heart.

But to you as a mass I speak this. If you will be blessed under the Word, would that you would pray before you come here. You sometimes hear of preparation for the Lord's Supper—I am sure if the Word is to be blessed, there ought to be a preparation for hearing it. Do you, when you come up to this house, pray to God before you come, "Lord, give the minister words; help him to speak to me today. Lord, save me today. May the Word today be a quickening word to my poor soul"? Ah! My friends, you would never go without the blessing if you come up prayerfully looking for it, having asked it of God.

Then after prayer, if you would be blessed under the Word, there should be an expectation of being blessed. It is wonderful the differences between the same sermon preached in different places, and I do not doubt that the same words uttered by different men would have different effects. With some men the hearers expect they will say something worth hearing. They listen, and the man does say something worth hearing. Another man might say just the same; nobody receives it as other than commonplace. Now if you can come up to the house of God expecting that there will be something for you, you will have it. We always get what we angle for. If we come up to find fault, there always will be faults to find. If we come up to get good, good will be gotten. God will send no man empty away; he shall have what he came for. If he came merely for curiosity, he shall have his curiosity gratified. If he came for good, he shall not be disappointed. We may be disappointed at man's door; we never were at God's. Man may send us away empty, but God never will.

Then while listening to the Word with expectation, it will naturally come to pass that you will listen with deep attention. A young boy who had been awakened to a sense of sin was remarked to be exceedingly attentive to sermons, and when asked why it was, he said, "Because I do not know which part of the sermon may be blessed to me, but I know that whichever it is, the devil will do his utmost to take my attention off then for fear I should be blessed." So he would listen to the whole of it, lest by any means the Word of life should be let slip. So do you, and you will certainly be in the way of being blessed by the Word.

Next to that, all through the sermon be appropriating it, saying to yourselves, "Does that belong to me?" If it be a promise, say, "Is that mine?" If it be a threatening, do not cover yourselves with the shield of hard-heartedness but say, "If that threatening belongs to me, let it have its full force on me." Sit under the sermon with your breasts open to the Word; be ready to let the arrow come in.

Above all, this will be of no avail unless you hear with faith. "Now faith comes by hearing." There must be faith mingled with the hearing. But you say, "What is faith? Is faith to believe that Christ died for me?" No, it is not. The Arminian says that faith is to believe that Christ died for you. He teaches in the first place that Christ died for everybody, therefore, he says, he died for you. Of course he died for everybody, and if he died for everybody he must have died for you. That is not faith at all.

I hold, on the other hand, that Christ died for believers, that he died for no man that will be lost, that all he died for will be saved, that his intention cannot be frustrated in any man, that if he died to save any man, that man will be saved. Your question today is not whether Christ died for you or not, but it is this: The Scripture says, "Believe on the Lord Jesus Christ and you shall be saved." And what is it to believe? To believe is to trust it is the same word, though believe is not so plain a word as trust. To trust Christ is to believe. I feel I cannot save myself, that all my doings and feelings cannot save me; I trust Christ to save me. That is faith, and the moment I trust Christ, I then know that Christ died for me, for they who trust him he has surely died to save, so surely he died to save them that he will save them, so finished his work that he will never lose them, according to his own Word; "Give unto my sheep eternal life, and they shall never perish, neither shall any pluck them out of my hand."

"But may I trust it!" says one. May! You are commanded to do it. "But I dare not." What! Dare not do what God bids you! Rather say, "I dare not live without Christ, I dare not disobey." God has said, "This is the commandment, that you believe on the Lord Jesus Christ whom he has sent." This is the great commandment sent to you. Today trust Christ and you are saved; disobey that command, and do what you will, you are damned.

Go home to your chamber and say unto God, "I desire to believe what I have heard; l desire to trust my immortal soul in Jesus's hands. Give me genuine faith; give me a real trust. Save me now and save me hereafter." I dare avow it—I never can believe that any man so hearing the Word can by any possibility perish. Hear it, receive it, pray over it, and trust Christ through it, and if you are lost, there can be none saved.

If this foundation give way, another can never be laid. If you fall, we all fall together. If trusting in Christ you can perish, all God's prophets, martyrs, confessors, and ministers perish too. You cannot. He will never fail you; trust him now.

Spirit of God, incline the hearts of men to trust Christ. Enable them now to overcome their pride and their timidity, and may they trust the Savior now, and they are saved forever through Jesus Christ our Lord. Amen.

Preach the Gospel[15]

"For though I preach the gospel, I have nothing to glory of: for necessity is laid upon me; yea, woe is unto me, if I preach not the gospel!"
(1 Corinthians 9:16)

The greatest man of apostolic times was the apostle Paul. He was always great in everything. If you consider him as a sinner, he was exceeding sinful. If you regard him as a persecutor, he was exceeding mad against the Christians and persecuted them even unto strange cities. If you take him as a convert, his conversion was the most notable one of

---

15. Published in *Metropolitan Tabernacle Pulpit*, Vol. 1 in 1855 by Charles Spurgeon. This is sermon 34, delivered on August 5, 1855.

which we read, worked by miraculous power and by the direct voice of Jesus speaking from heaven: Saul, Saul, why do you persecute me?" If we take him simply as a Christian, he was an extraordinary one, loving his Master more than others and seeking more than others to exemplify the grace of God in his life. But if you take him as an apostle and as a preacher of the Word, he stands out pre-eminent as the prince of preachers and a preacher to kings—for he preached before Agrippa, before Nero Caesar—he stood before emperors and kings for Christ's name's sake.

It was the characteristic of Paul that, whatever he did, he did with all his heart. He was one of the men who could not allow one half of his frame to be exercised while the other half was indolent, but when he set to work, the whole of his energies—every nerve, every sinew—were strained in the work to be done, be it bad work or be it good. Paul, therefore, could speak from experience concerning his ministry, because he was the chief of ministers. There is no nonsense in what he speaks; it is all from the depth of his soul. And we may be sure that when he wrote this, he wrote it with a strong, unpalsied hand, "Though I preach the gospel, I have nothing to glory of: for necessity is laid upon me; yea, woe is me, if I preach not the gospel."[16]

---

16. 1 Corinthians 9:16.

Now these words of Paul, I trust, are applicable to many ministers in the present day, to all those who are especially called, who are directed by the inward impulse of the Holy Spirit to occupy the position of gospel ministers. In trying to consider this verse, we shall have three inquiries this morning: First, What is it to preach the gospel? Secondly, Why is it that a minister has nothing to glorify of? And thirdly, What is that necessity and that woe, of which it is written, "Necessity is laid upon me, yea, woe is unto me if I preach not the gospel?"

What Is It to Preach the Gospel?

There are a variety of opinions concerning this question, and possibly amongst my own audience—though I believe we are very uniform in our doctrinal sentiments—there might be found two or three very ready answers to this question: What is it to preach the gospel? I shall therefore attempt to answer it myself according to my own judgment, if God will help me; and if it does not happen to be the correct answer, you are at liberty to supply a better to yourselves at home.

The first answer I shall give to the question is this: To preach the gospel is to state every doctrine contained in God's Word and to give every truth its proper prominence. Men may preach a part of the gospel; they may only preach one single doctrine of it. And I would not say that a man did not preach the gospel at all if he did but maintain the doctrine of justification by faith—"By grace are you saved through faith."[17] I should put him down for a gospel minister, but not for one who preached the whole gospel. No man can be said to preach the whole gospel of God if he leaves out, knowingly and intentionally, one single truth of the blessed God. This remark of mine must be a very cutting one and ought to strike into the consciences of many who make it almost a matter of principle to keep back certain truths from the people because they are afraid of them.

In conversation a week or two ago with an eminent professor, he said to me, "Sir, we know that we ought not to preach the doctrine of election, because it is not calculated to convert sinners." "But," said I to him, "who is the men that dares to find fault with the truth of God? You admit with me that it is a truth, and yet you say it must not be preached. I dare not have said that thing. I should reckon it supreme arrogance to have ventured to say that a doctrine ought not to be preached when the all-wise God has seen fit to reveal it. Besides, is the whole gospel intended to convert sinners? There are some truths that God blesses to

---

17. Ephesians 2:8.

98

the conversion of sinners; but are there not other portions that were intended for the comfort of the saint? And ought not these to be a subject of gospel ministry as well as the others? And shall I look at one and disregard the other? No. If God says, 'Comfort you, comfort you, my people,' if election comforts God's people, then must I preach it."

But I am not quite so sure that, after all, that doctrine is not calculated to convert sinners. For the great Jonathan Edwards tells us that in the greatest excitement of one of his revivals, he preached the sovereignty of God in the salvation or condemnation of man and showed that God was infinitely just if he sent men to hell, that he was infinitely merciful if he saved any, and that it was all of his own free grace. And he said, "I found no doctrine caused more thought, nothing entered more deeply into the heart than the proclamation of that truth."

The same might be said of other doctrines. There are certain truths in God's Word that are condemned to silence; they, forsooth, are not to be uttered because, according to the theories of certain persons, they are not calculated to promote certain ends. But is it for me to judge God's truth? Am I to put his words in the scale, and say, "This is good, and that is evil?" Am I to take God's Bible and sever it and say, "This is husk, and this is wheat?" Am I to cast away any one truth and say, "I dare not preach it"? No; God forbid. Whatsoever is written in God's Word is written for our instruction, and the whole of it is profitable, either for reproof, for consolation, or for edification in righteousness. No truth of God's Word ought to be withheld, but every portion of it preached in its own proper order.

Some men purposely confine themselves to four or five topics continually. Should you step into their chapel, you would naturally expect to hear them preaching either from this, "Not of the will of the flesh, but of the will of God," or else, "Elect according to the foreknowledge of God the Father." You know that the moment you step in you are sure to hear nothing but election and high doctrine that day. Such men err also, quite as much as others, if they give too great prominence to one truth to the neglect of the others. Whatsoever is here to be preached, "all of it, whatever name you please, write it high, write it low—the Bible, the whole Bible, and nothing but the Bible is the standard of the true Christian."

Alas! Alas! Many make an iron ring of their doctrines, and he who dares to step beyond that narrow circle is not reckoned orthodox. God bless heretics, then! God send us more of them! Many make theology into a kind of treadwheel consisting of five doctrines that are everlastingly rotated, for they never go on to anything else. There ought to be every truth preached. And if God has written in his Word that "he who believes not is condemned already," that is as much to be preached as the truth that "there is no condemnation to them that are in Jesus Christ." If I find it written, "O Israel, you have destroyed thyself," that man's condemnation is his own fault, I am to preach that as well as the next clause, "in me is your help found."

We ought, each of us who are entrusted with the ministry, to seek to preach all truth. I know it may be impossible to tell you all of it. That high hill of truth has mists upon its summit. No mortal eye can see its pinnacle, nor has the foot of man ever trodden it. But yet let us paint the mist if we cannot paint the summit. Let us depict the difficulty itself if we cannot unravel it. Let us not hide anything, but if the mountain of truth be cloudy at the top, let us say, "Clouds and darkness are around him." Let us not deny it, and let us not think of cutting down the mountain to our own standard because we cannot see its summit or cannot reach its pinnacle. He who would preach the gospel must preach all the gospel. He who would have it said he is a faithful minister must not keep back any part of revelation.

Again, am I asked what it is to preach the gospel. I answer to preach the gospel is to exalt Jesus

Christ. Perhaps this is the best answer that I could give. I am very sorry to see very often how little the gospel is understood even by some of the best Christians. Some time ago there was a young woman under great distress of soul. She came to a very pious Christian man, who said, "My dear girl, you must go home and pray." Well, I thought within myself, that is not the Bible way at all. It never says, "Go home and pray."

The poor girl went home; she did pray, and she still continued in distress. Said he, "You must wait, you must read the Scriptures and study them." That is not the Bible way; that is not exalting Christ. I find a great many preachers are preaching that kind of doctrine. They tell a poor convinced sinner, "You must go home and pray and read the Scriptures; you must attend the ministry," and so on. Works, works, works—instead of "By grace are you saved through faith." If a penitent should come and ask me, "What must I do to be saved?" I would say, "Christ must save you—believe on the name of the Lord Jesus Christ."

I would neither direct to prayer, nor reading of the Scriptures, nor attending God's house but simply direct to faith, naked faith on God's gospel. Not that I despise prayer—that must come after faith. Not that I speak a word against the searching of the Scriptures— that is an infallible mark of God's children. Not that

I find fault with attendance on God's Word—God forbid! I love to see people there. But none of those things are the way of salvation. It is nowhere written, "He who attends chapel shall be saved," or "He who reads the Bible shall be saved." Nor do I read, "He who prays and is baptized shall be saved" but "He who believes"—he who has a naked faith on the "man Christ Jesus"—on his Godhead, on his manhood—is delivered from sin. To preach that faith alone saves is to preach God's truth. Nor will I for one moment concede to any man the name of a gospel minister if he preaches anything as the plan of salvation except faith in Jesus Christ, faith, faith, nothing but faith in his name.

But we are, most of us, very much muddled in our ideas. We get so much work stored into our brain, such an idea of merit and of doing wrought into our hearts, that it is almost impossible for us to preach justification by faith clearly and fully. And when we do, our people won't receive it. We tell them, "Believe on the name of the Lord Jesus Christ and you shall be saved." But they have a notion that faith is something so wonderful, so mysterious that it is quite impossible that without doing something else they can ever get it. Now, that faith that unites to the Lamb is an instantaneous gift of God, and he who believes on the

Lord Jesus is that moment saved without anything else whatsoever.

Ah! My friends, do we not want more exalting Christ in our preaching, and more exalting Christ in our living? Poor Mary said, "They have taken away my Lord and I know not where they have laid him." And she might say so now-a-days if she could rise from the grave. Oh! To have a Christ-exalting ministry! Oh! To have preaching that magnifies Christ in his person, that extols his divinity, that loves his humanity; to have preaching that shows him as prophet, priest, and king to his people! To have preaching whereby the spirit manifests the Son of God unto his children; to have preaching that says, "Look unto him and be you saved all the ends of the earth." Calvary preaching, Calvary theology, Calvary books, Calvary sermons! These are the things we want, and in proportion as we have Calvary exalted and Christ magnified, the gospel is preached in our midst.

The third answer to the question is that to preach the gospel is to give every class of character his due. "You are only to preach to God's dear people if you go into that pulpit," said a deacon once to a minister. Said the minister, "Have you marked them all on the back that I may know them?" What is the good of this large chapel if I am only to preach to God's dear people? They are few enough. God's dear people might be held in the vestry. We have many more here besides God's dear people, and how am I to be sure, if I am told to preach only to God's dear people, that somebody else won't take it to himself?

At another time someone might say, "Now, be sure you preach to sinners. If you do not preach to sinners this morning, you won't preach the gospel. We shall only hear you once, and we shall be sure you are not right if you do not happen to preach to sinners this particular morning in this particular sermon." What nonsense, my friends! There are times when the children must be fed, and there are times when the sinner must be warned. There are different times for different objects. If a man is preaching to God's saints and if it so happens that little is said to sinners, is he to be blamed for it, provided that at another time when he is not comforting the saints he directs his attention specially to the ungodly?

I heard a good remark from an intelligent friend of mine the other day. A person was finding fault with *Dr. Hawker's Morning and Evening Portions* because they were not calculated to convert sinners. He said to the gentleman, "Did you ever read *Grote's History of Greece?*"

"Yes." Well, that is a shocking book, is it not? For it is not calculated to convert sinners.

"Yes, but," said the other, "*Grote's History of Greece* was never meant to convert sinners."

"No," said my friend, "and if you had read the preface to *Dr. Hawker's Morning and Evening Portions*, you would see that it was never meant to convert sinners but to feed God's people, and if it answers its end, the man has been wise, though he has not aimed at some other end."

Every class of person is to have his due. He who preaches solely to saints at all times does not preach the gospel. He who preaches solely and only to the sinner, and never to the saint, does not preach the whole of the gospel. We have amalgamation here. We have the saint who is full of assurance and strong. We have the saint who is weak and low in faith. We have the young convert. We have the man halting between two opinions. We have the moral man. We have the sinner. We have the reprobate. We have the outcast. Let each have a word. Let each have a portion of meat in due season, not at every season but in due season. He who omits one class of character does not know how to preach the entire gospel.

What! Am I to be put into the pulpit and to be told that I am to confine myself to certain truths only, to comfort God's saints? I will not have it so. God gives men hearts to love their fellow creatures, and are they to have no development for that heart? If I love the ungodly, am I to have no means of speaking to them? May I not tell them of judgment to come, of righteousness, and of their sin? God forbid I should so stultify my nature and so brutalize myself as to have a tearless eye when I consider the loss of my fellow creatures and to stand and say "You are dead, I have nothing to say to you!" And to preach in effect if not in words that most damnable heresy, that if men are to be saved they will be saved—that if they are not to be saved they will not be saved; that necessarily they must sit still and do nothing whatever and that it matters not whether they live in sin or in righteousness. Some strong fate has bound them down with adamantine chains, and their destiny is so certain that they may live on in sin.

I believe their destiny is certain—that as elect, they will be saved, and if not elect they are damned forever. But I do not believe the heresy that follows as an inference that therefore men are irresponsible and may sit still. That is a heresy against which I have ever protested as being a doctrine of the devil and not of God at all. We believe in destiny; we believe in predestination; we believe in election and non-election: but, notwithstanding that, we believe that we must preach to men, "Believe on the Lord Jesus Christ and you shall be saved," but believe not on him and you are damned.

I had thought of giving one more answer to this question, but time fails me. The answer would have been somewhat like this—that to preach the gospel is not to preach certain truths about the gospel, not to preach about the people, but to preach to the people. To preach the gospel is not to talk about what the gospel is, but to preach it into the heart, not by your own might but by the influence of the Holy Spirit. Not to stand and talk as if we were speaking to the angel Gabriel and telling him certain things, but to speak as man to man and pour our heart in to our fellow's heart. This, I take it, is to preach the gospel, and not to mumble some dry manuscript over on Sunday morning or Sunday evening.

To preach the gospel is not to send a curate to do your duty for you; it is not to put on your fine gown and then stand and give out some lofty speculation. To preach the gospel is not, with the hands of a bishop, to turn over some beautiful specimen of prayer and then to go down again and leave it to some humbler person to speak. Nay. To preach the gospel is to proclaim with trumpet tongue and flaming zeal the unsearchable riches of Christ Jesus so that men may hear, and understanding, may turn to God with full purpose of heart. This is to preach the gospel.

How Are Ministers Not Allowed to Glory?

The second question is, How is it that ministers are not allowed to glory? "For though I preach the gospel, I have nothing to glorify it." There are some weeds that will grow anywhere, and one of them is pride. Pride will grow on a rock as well as in a garden. Pride will grow in the heart of a shoe-black as well as in the heart of an alderman. Pride will grow in the heart of a servant girl and equally as well in the heart of her mistress. And pride will grow in the pulpit. It is a weed that is dreadfully rampant. It wants cutting down every week, or else we should stand up to our knees in it.

This pulpit is a shocking bad soil for pride. It grows terribly, and I scarcely know whether you ever find a preacher of the gospel who will not confess that he has the greatest temptation to pride. I suppose that even those ministers of whom nothing is said but that they are very good people who have a city church with some six people attending it, have a temptation to pride. But whether that is so or not, I am quite sure wherever there is a large assembly, and wherever a great deal of noise and stir is made concerning any man, there is a great danger of pride.

And, mark you, the more proud a man is, the greater will be his fall at last. If people will hold a minister up in their hands and do not keep hold of him but let him go, what a fall he will have, poor fellow, when it is all over. It has been so with many. Many men have been held up by the arms of men, they have been held up by the arms of praise and not of prayer; these arms have become weak, and down they have fallen. I say there is temptation to pride in the pulpit, but there is no ground for it in the pulpit; there is no soil for pride to grow on, but it will grow without any. "I have nothing to glorify of." But, notwithstanding, there often comes in some reason why we should glory, not real, but apparent to ourselves.

Now, how is it that a true minister feels he has "nothing to glorify of"? First, because he is very conscious of his own imperfections. I think no man will ever form a more just opinion of himself than he who is called constantly and incessantly to preach. Some man once thought he could preach, and on being allowed to enter the pulpit he found his words did not come quite so freely as he expected, and in the utmost trepidation and fear he leaned over the front of the pulpit and said "My friends, if you would come up here, it would take the conceit out of you all. I verily believe it would out of a great many, could they once try themselves whether they could preach. It would take their critical conceit out of them and make them think that after all it was not such easy work." He who preaches best feels that he preaches worst. He who has set up some lofty model in his own mind of what eloquence should be and what earnest appeal ought to be will know how much he falls below it. He, best of all, can reprove himself when he knows his own deficiency.

I do not believe when a man does a thing well, that therefore he will glory in it. On the other hand, I think that he will be the best judge of his own imperfections and will see them most clearly. He knows what he ought to be; other men do not. They stare and gaze and think it is wonderful when he thinks it is wonderfully absurd and retires wondering that he has not done better. Every true minister will feel that he is deficient. He will compare himself with such men as Whitfield, with such preachers as those of puritanical times, and he will say, "What am I? Like a dwarf beside a giant, an ant hill by the side of the mountain."

When he retires to rest on Sabbath night, he will toss from side to side on his bed because he feels that he has missed the mark, that he has not had that earnestness, that solemnity, that death-like intenseness of purpose that became his position. He will accuse himself of not having dwelt enough on this point, or for having shunned the other, or not having been explicit enough on some certain subject, or expanded another too much. He will see his own faults, for God always chastises his own children at nighttime when they have done something wrong. We need not others to reprove us; God himself takes us in hand. The most highly honored before God will often feel himself dishonored in his own esteem.

Again, another means of causing us to cease from all glory is the fact that God reminds us that all our gifts are borrowed. And strikingly have I this morning been reminded of that great truth—that all our gifts are borrowed, by reading in a newspaper to the following effect:

> Last week, the quiet neighborhood of New Town was much disturbed by an occurrence which has thrown a gloom over the entire neighborhood. A gentleman of considerable attainment, who has won an honorable degree at the university has for some months been deranged. He had kept an academy for young gentlemen, but his insanity had obliged him to desist from his occupation, and he has for some time lived alone in a house in the neighborhood. The landlord obtained a warrant of ejectment; and it being found necessary to handcuff him, he was, by sad mismanagement,

compelled to remain on the steps, exposed to the gaze of a great crowd, until at last a vehicle arrived, which conveyed him to the asylum. One of his pupils (says the paper) is Mr. Spurgeon.

The man from whom I learned whatever of human learning I have has now become a raving lunatic in the asylum! When I saw that, I felt I could bend my knee with humble gratitude and thank my God that not yet had my reason reeled, not yet had those powers departed. Oh! How thankful we ought to be that our talents are preserved to us and that our mind is not gone! Nothing came nearer and closer to me than that. There was one who had taken all pains with me—a man of genius and of ability, and yet there he is! How fallen! How fallen! How speedily does human nature come from its high estate and sink below the level of the brutes?

Bless God, my friends, for your talents! Thank him for your reason! Thank him for your intellect! Simple as it may be, it is enough for you, and if you lost it, you would soon mark the difference. Take heed to yourself lest in aught you say. "This is Babylon that I have built," for, remember, both trowel and mortar must come from him. The life, the voice, the talent, the imagination, the eloquence—all are the gift of God. And he who has the greatest gifts must feel that unto God belong the shield of the mighty, for he has given might to his people and strength unto his servants.

Another means whereby God preserves his ministers from glorying is this: He makes them feel their constant dependance upon the Holy Spirit. Some do not feel it, I confess. Some will venture to preach without the Spirit of God or without entreating him. But I think that no man who is really commissioned from on high will ever venture to do so, but he will feel that he needs the Spirit.

Once, while preaching in Scotland, the Spirit of God was pleased to desert me. I could not speak as usually I have done. I was obliged to tell the people that the chariot wheels were taken off and that the chariot dragged very heavily along. I have felt the benefit of that ever since. It humbled me bitterly, for I could have crept into a nutshell, and I would have hidden myself in any obscure corner of the earth. I felt as if I should speak no more in the name of the Lord, and then the thought came "Oh! You are an ungrateful creature. Has not God spoken by you hundreds of times? And this once when he would not do so, will you upbraid him for it? Nay, rather thank him that a hundred times he has stood by you, and, if once he has forsaken you, admire his goodness that thus he would keep you humble."

Some may imagine that want of study brought me into that condition, but I can honestly affirm, that it was not so. I think that I am bound to give myself unto reading and not tempt the Spirit by unthought-of effusions. Usually I deem it a duty to seek a sermon of my Master and implore him to impress it on my mind, but on that occasion I think I had even prepared more carefully then than I ordinarily do, so that unpreparedness was not the reason. The simple fact was this: "The wind blows where it desires," and winds do not always blow hurricanes. Sometimes the winds themselves are still. And therefore, if I rest on the Spirit, I cannot expect I should always feel its power alike.

What could I do without the celestial influence, for to that I owe everything? By this thought God humbles his servants. God will teach us how much we want it. He will not let us think we are doing anything ourselves. "Nay," says he, "you shall have none of the glory. I will take you down. Are you thinking 'I am doing this'? I will show you what you are without me." Out goes Samson. He attacks the Philistines. He fancies he can slay them, but they are on him. His eyes are out. His glory is gone because he trusted not in his God but rested in himself. Every minister will be made to feel his dependence upon the Spirit, and then will he with emphasis say, as Paul did, "If I preach the gospel, I have nothing to glorify of."

What is That Necessity Laid upon Us to Preach the Gospel?

Now comes the third question, with which we are to finish: What is that necessity laid upon us to preach your gospel? First, a very great part of that necessity springs from the call itself: If a man be truly called of God to the ministry, I will defy him to withhold himself from it. A man who has really within him the inspiration of the Holy Spirit calling him to preach cannot help it. He must preach. As fire within the bones, so will that influence be until it blazes forth. Friends may check him, foes criticize him, despisers sneer at him, but the man is indomitable; he must preach if he has the call of heaven. All earth might forsake him, but he would preach to the barren mountaintops. If he has the call of heaven, if he has no congregation he would preach to the rippling waterfalls and let the brooks hear his voice. He could not be silent. He would become a voice crying in the wilderness, "Prepare you the way of the Lord."

I no more believe it possible to stop ministers than to stop the stars of heaven. I think it no more possible to make a man cease from preaching, if he is really called, than to stop some mighty cataract by seeking, with an infant's cup, to drink its waters. The man has been moved of heaven, who shall stop him? He has been touched of God, who shall impede him? With an eagle's wing he must fly; who shall chain him to the earth? With seraph's voice he must speak, who shall stop his lips? Is not his word like a fire within me? Must I not speak if God has placed it there? And when a man does speak as the Spirit gives him utterance, he will feel a holy joy akin to heaven; and when it is over he wishes to be at his work again and longs to be once more preaching. I do not think young men are called of God to any great work who preach once a week and think they have done their duty. I think if God has called a man, he will impel him to be more or less constantly at it, and he will feel that he must preach among the nations the unsearchable riches of Christ.

But another thing will make us preach: We shall feel that woe is unto us if we preach not the gospel, and that is the sad destitution of this poor fallen world. Oh, minister of the gospel! Stand for one moment and think of your poor fellow creatures! See them like a stream, rushing to eternity—ten thousand to their endless home each solemn moment fly! See the termination of that stream, that tremendous cataract that dashes streams of souls into the pit! Oh, minister, think that men are being damned each hour by thousands and that each time your pulse beats another soul lifts up its eyes in hell, being in torments. Think how men are speeding on their way to destruction, how "the love of many waxes cold" and "iniquity does abound." I say, is there not a necessity laid upon you? Is it not woe unto you if you preach not the gospel?

Take your walk one evening through the streets of London when the dusk has gathered and darkness veils the people. Mark you not the profligate hurrying on to her accursed work? See you not thousands and tens of thousands annually ruined? Up from the hospital and the asylum there comes a voice, "Woe is unto you if you preach not the gospel." Go to that huge place built around with massive walls, enter the dungeons, and see the thieves who have for years spent their lives in sin. Wend your way sometimes to that sad square of Newgate and see the murderer hanged. A voice shall come from each house of correction, from each prison, from each gallows, saying, "Woe is unto you if you preach not the gospel." Go you to the thousand deathbeds and mark how men are perishing in ignorance, not knowing the ways of God. See their terror as they approach their Judge, never having known what it was to be saved, not even knowing the way. And as you see them quivering before their Maker, hear a voice, "Minister, woe is unto you if you preach not the gospel."

Or take another course. Travel round this great metropolis and stop at the door of some place where there is heard the tinkling of bells, chanting, and music, but where the whore of Babylon has her sway, and lies are preached for truth. And when you come home and think of Popery and Puseyism, let a voice come to you, "Minister, woe is unto you if you preach not the gospel." Or step into the hall of the infidel where he blasphemes your Maker's name, or sit in the theater where plays libidinous and loose are acted, and from all these haunts of vice there comes the voice, "Minister, woe is unto you if you preach not the gospel."

And take your last solemn walk down to the chambers of the lost; let the abyss of hell be visited, and stand you and hear "The sullen groans, the hollow moans, And shrieks of tortured Spirits." Put your ear at hell's gate, and for a little while listen to the commingled screams and shrieks of agony and fell despair that shall lend you ear. And as you come from that sad place with that doleful music still affrighting you, you will hear the voice, "Minister! minister! Woe is unto you if you preach not the gospel." Only let us have these things before our eyes, and we must preach.

Stop preaching! Stop preaching! Let the sun stop shining, and we will preach in darkness. Let the waves stop their ebb and flow, and still our voice shall preach the gospel. Let the world stop its revolutions, let the planets stay their motion; we will still preach the gospel. Until the fiery center of this earth shall burst through the thick ribs of her brazen mountains, we shall still preach the gospel. Till the universal conflagration shall dissolve the earth and matter shall be swept away, these lips, or the lips of some others called of God, shall still thunder forth the voice of Yahweh. We cannot help it. Necessity is laid upon us, yea woe is unto us if we preach not the gospel.

Now, my dear hearers, one word with you. There are some persons in this audience who are verily guilty in the sight of God because they do not preach the gospel. I cannot think out of the fifteen hundred or two thousand persons now present, within the reach of my voice, there are none who are qualified to preach the gospel besides myself. I have not so bad an opinion of you as to conceive myself to be superior in intellect to one half of you, or even in the power of preaching God's Word. And even supposing I should be, I cannot believe that I have such a congregation that there are not among you many who have gifts and talents that qualify you to preach the Word.

Among the Scotch Baptists it is the custom to call upon all the brothers to exhort on the Sabbath morning. They have no regular minister to preach on that occasion, but every man preaches who likes to get up and speak. That is all very well, only, I fear, many unqualified brothers would be the greatest speakers, since it is a known fact that men who have little to say will often keep on the longest. And if I were chairman, I should say, "Brother, it is written, 'Speak to edification.' I am sure you would not edify yourself and your wife. You had better go and try that first, and if you cannot succeed, don't waste our precious time."

But still I say, I cannot conceive but what there are some here this morning who are flowers "wasting their sweetness in the desert air," "gems of purest ray serene" lying in the dark caverns of ocean's oblivion. This is a very serious question. If there be any talent in the church at Park Street, let it be developed. If there be any preachers in my congregation, let them preach. Many ministers make it a point to check young men in this respect. There is my hand, such as it is, to help any one of you if you think you can tell sinners round what a dear Savior you have found. I would like to find scores of preachers among you; would to God that all the Lord's servants were prophets. There are some here who ought to be prophets, only they are half-afraid—well, we must devise some scheme of getting rid of their bashfulness. I cannot bear to think that while the devil sets all his servants to work there should be one servant of Jesus Christ asleep.

Young man, go home and examine yourself, see what your abilities are, and if you find that you have ability, then try in some poor humble room to tell to a dozen poor people what they must do to be saved. You need not aspire to become absolutely and solely dependent upon the ministry, but if it should please God, even desire it. He that desires a bishopric desires a good thing. At any rate, seek in some way to be preaching the gospel of God. I have preached this sermon especially because I want to commence a movement from this place that shall reach others. I want to find some in my church, if it be possible, who will preach the gospel. And mark you, if you have talent and power, woe is unto you if you preach not the gospel.

But oh! My friends, if it is woe unto us if we preach not the gospel, what is the woe unto you if you hear and receive not the gospel? May God give us both to escape from that woe! May the gospel of God be unto us the savor of life unto life and not of death unto death.

The Word of the Cross[18]

"For the preaching of the cross is to them
that perish foolishness; but unto us which
are saved it is the power of God."
(1 Corinthians 1:18)

Note well that in the seventeenth verse Paul had renounced the "wisdom of words." He says that he was sent to preach the gospel, "not with wisdom of words, lest the cross of Christ should be made of none effect." It is very clear, therefore, that there is an excellence, elegance, and eloquence of language that would deprive the gospel of its due effect. I have never yet

18. Published in *Metropolitan Tabernacle Pulpit*, Vol. 27 in 1881 by Charles Spurgeon. This is sermon 1611, delivered on July 31, 1881.

heard that the cross of Christ was made of none effect by great plainness of speech, nor even by ruggedness of language, but it is the "wisdom of words" that is said to have this destroying power. Oh, dreadful wisdom of words! God grant that we may be delivered from making attempts at it, for we ought earnestly to shun anything and everything that can be so mischievous in its influence as to make the cross of Christ of none effect.

The "wisdom of words" works evil at times by veiling the truth that ought to be set forth in the clearest possible manner. The doctrine of atonement by blood, which is the essence of the preaching of the cross, is objectionable to many minds, and hence certain preachers take care not to state it too plainly. Prudently, as they call it—craftily, as the apostle Paul would call it—they tone down the objectionable features of the great sacrifice, hoping by pretty phrases somewhat to remove the "offense of the cross." Proud minds object to substitution, which is the very edge of the doctrine; hence theories are adopted that leave out the idea of laying sin upon the Savior and making him to be a curse for us. Self-sacrifice is set forth as possessing a high, heroic influence by which we are stimulated to self-salvation, but the Lord's suffering as the just for the unjust is not mentioned. The cross in such a case is not at all the cross by which self-condemned sinners can be comforted and the hardened can be subdued, but quite another matter. Those who thus veil an unwelcome truth imagine that they make disciples, whereas they are only paying homage to unbelief and comforting men in their rejection of the divine propitiation for sin. Whatever the preacher may mean in his heart, he will be guilty of the blood of souls if he does not clearly proclaim a real sacrifice for sin.

Too often the "wisdom of words" explains the gospel away. It is possible to refine a doctrine till the very soul of it is gone; you may draw such nice distinctions that the true meaning is filtered away. Certain divines tell us that they must adapt truth to the advance of the age, which means that they must murder it and fling its dead body to the dogs. It is asserted that the advanced philosophy of the nineteenth century requires a progressive theology to keep abreast of it, which simply means that a popular lie shall take the place of an offensive truth. Under pretense of winning the cultured intellects of the age, "the wisdom of words" has gradually landed us in a denial of those first principles for which the martyrs died. Apologies for the gospel, in which the essence of it is conceded to the unbeliever, are worse than infidelity. I hate that defense of the gospel that razes it to the ground to preserve it from destruction.

The "wisdom of words," however, is more frequently used with the intent of adorning the gospel and making it to appear somewhat more beautiful than it would be in its natural form. They would paint the rose and enamel the lily, add whiteness to snow and brightness to the sun. With their wretched candles they would help us to see the stars. O superfluity of naughtiness! The cross of Christ is sublimely simple; to adorn it is to dishonor it. There is no statement under heaven more musical than this: "God was in Christ reconciling the world unto himself, not imputing their trespasses unto them." All the bells that you could ring to make it more harmonious would only add a jingle jangle to its heavenly melody, which is in itself so sweet that it charms the harpers before the throne of God.

The doctrine that God descended upon the earth in human nature and in that nature bore our sins, carried our sorrows, and made expiation for our transgressions by the death of the cross is in itself matchless poetry, the perfection of all that is ennobling in thought and creed. Yet the attempt is made to decorate the gospel, as though it needed somewhat to commend it to the understanding and the heart. The result is that men's minds are attracted from the gospel either to the preacher or to some utterly indifferent point. Hearers carry home charming morsels of poetry, but they forget the precious blood. They recollect the elaborate metaphors so daintily wrought out, but they forget the five wounds and fail to look unto the Lord Jesus and be saved. The truth is buried under flowers.

Brothers, let us cut out of our sermons everything that takes men's minds away from the cross. One look at Jesus is better than the most attentive gazing at our gems of speech. One of the old masters found that certain vases he had depicted upon the sacramental table attracted more notice than the face of the Lord, whom he had painted sitting at the head of the feast, and therefore he struck them out at once. Let us, my brothers, do the same whenever anything of ours withdraws the mind from Jesus. Christ must ever be in the foreground, and our sermons must point to him, or they will do more harm than good. We must preach Christ crucified and set him forth like the sun in the heavens as the sole light of men.

Some seem to imagine that the gospel does not contain within itself sufficient force for its own spreading, and therefore they dream that if it is to have power among men it must either be through the logical way in which it is put—in which case all glory be to logic—or through the handsome manner in which it is stated—in which case all glory be to rhetoric. The notion is current that we should seek the aid of prestige, talent, novelty, or excitement, for the gospel itself, the doctrine of the cross, is impotent in its hands and lame upon its feet and must be sustained by outside power and carried as by a nurse wherever it would go. Reason, elocution, art, music, or some other force must introduce and support it, or it will make no advance—so some injuriously dream.

That is not Paul's notion; he speaks of the cross of Christ as being itself the power of God, and he says that it is to be preached "not with wisdom of words," lest the power should be attributed to the aforesaid wisdom of words and the cross of Christ should be proven to have in itself no independent power or, in other words, to be of none effect. Paul would not thus degrade the cross for a moment, and therefore, though qualified to dispute with schoolmen and philosophers, he disdained to dazzle with arguments and sophistries. And though he himself could speak with masterly energy—let his epistles bear witness to that—yet he used great plainness of speech, that the force of his teaching might lie in the doctrine itself and not in his language, style, or delivery. He was jealous of the honor of the cross and would not spread it by any force but its own, even as he says in the fourth and fifth verses of the second chapter of this epistle, "My speech and my preaching was not with enticing words of man's wisdom, but in demonstration of the Spirit and of power, that your faith should not stand in the wisdom of men, but in the power of God."

Having cleared our way of the wisdom of words, we now come to the word of wisdom. Paul preached the cross, and our first head shall be the word of the cross. Many give the cross a bad word, and so our second head shall be the word of its despisers concerning it; they called it foolishness: and then, thirdly, we will think upon the word applied to the cross by those who believe it; it is to them "the power of God." O that the Holy Spirit may use it as the power of God to all of us this day.

The Word of the Cross

I borrow the term from the Revised Version, which runs thus: "The word of the cross is to them that are perishing foolishness, but unto us who are being saved it is the power of God." This is, to my mind, an accurate translation. The original is not "the preaching of the cross" but "the word of the cross." This rendering gives us a heading for our first division and at the same time brings before us exactly what the gospel is. It is "the word of the cross."

From which I gather, first, that the cross has one uniform teaching, or word. We are always to preach the word of the cross, and the cross has not many words, but one. There are not two gospels any more than there are two Gods. There are not two atonements any more than there are two Saviors. There is one gospel as there is one God, and there is one atonement as there is one Savior. Other gospels are not tolerated among earnest Christians.

What said the apostle? "If we or an angel from heaven preach any other gospel unto you than that which we have preached unto you, let him be candidly heard and quietly fraternized with." Nothing of the sort. I will quote the Scripture. Paul says, "Let him be accursed." He has no more tolerance than that for him, for Paul loved the souls of men, and to tolerate spiritual poison is to aid and abet the murder of souls. There is no gospel under heaven but the one gospel of Jesus Christ.

But what about other voices and other words? They are not voices from heaven nor words from God, for he has not in one place spoken one thing and in another place another. Neither is it according to the spirit of the gospel that there should be one form of gospel for the first six centuries and then another mood of it for the nineteenth century. Is it not written, "Jesus Christ, the same yesterday, today, and forever"? If the atonement were in progress, if the great sacrifice were not complete, then I could understand that there should be progress in the preaching of it.

But inasmuch as "It is finished" was pronounced by Christ upon the tree, and then he bowed his head and gave up the Spirit, there can be no further development in the fact or in the doctrine. Inasmuch as the word of the Lord which describes that atonement is so complete that he who adds thereunto shall have the plagues that are written in this book added unto him, I gather that there is no such thing as a progressive word of the cross but that the gospel is the same gospel today as it was when Paul in the beginning proclaimed it. The word of the cross, since it is the express word of God, endures forever. Generations of men come and go like yearly growths of the grass of the field, but the word of the Lord abides evermore the same in all places, the same to all nationalities, the same to all temperaments and constitutions of the mind. "Other foundation can no man lay than that which is laid."

From that word I gather, next, that the doctrine of the atonement is one word in contradistinction from many other words that are constantly being lettered. We preach Christ crucified, and his voice from the cross is, "Look unto me and be you saved." But another voice cries aloud, "Do this and you shall live." We know it; it is the voice of the old covenant that the Lord Jesus has removed, taking away the first covenant that he may establish the second. The doctrine of salvation by works, salvation by feelings, salvation by outward religiousness is not the word of the cross, which speaks in quite another fashion. The call to salvation by works is a strange voice within the fold of the church, and the sheep of Christ do not follow it, for they know not the voice of strangers. The word of the gospel speaks on this wise: "The word is near you, even in your mouth, and in your heart, that is, the word of faith, which we preach, that if you shall confess with your mouth the Lord Jesus and shall believe in your heart that God has raised him from the dead, you shall be saved." "Believe and live" is the word of the cross.

Much less do we regard the word of ceremonialism and priestcraft that still lingers among us. We had thought it was a dull echo of the dead past, but alas, it is a powerful voice and is constantly lifting up itself. Priestcraft is crying, "Confess to me and you shall have forgiveness. Perform this ceremony and undergo the other rite, and you shall receive a sacred benediction through men ordained of heaven." This voice we know not, for it is the voice of falsehood. He who believes in Christ Jesus has everlasting life. We are complete in him, and we know nothing of any priest save that one High Priest who by his one sacrifice has perfected forever them that are set apart.

Voices here and there are heard like mutterings from among the tombs; these are the maunderings of superstition, saying, "Lo, here," and "Lo, there," and one man has this revealed to him and another that, but to none of these have we any regard, for God hath spoken, and our preaching henceforth is nothing but "the word of the cross," which is none other than the word of the crucified Son of God who loved us and gave himself for us.

Brothers, let us hear this word of the cross, for in effect my text says, "Let the cross speak for itself." That is to be our preaching. We bid reasoning and speculation hold their tongues that the cross itself may speak. We let the cross speak its own word.

First, it cries aloud, God must be just. The dreadful voice of justice in its certainty and severity rings through the world in the sighs and cries and death groans of the Son of the Highest. Jesus has taken man's sin upon himself, and he must die for it, for be sin where it may, God must smite it. The Judge of all the earth must do right, and it is right that sin should involve suffering. Supreme justice must visit iniquity with death, and therefore Jesus on the cross, though in himself perfectly innocent and unspeakably lovely, must die the death, deserted by his Father because the iniquity of us all has been made to meet upon him. The cross cries unto the sons of men, "Oh, do not this abominable thing that God hates, for he will by no means spare the guilty." God must make bare my arm and bathe his sword in heaven to smite sin wherever it is found, for he smites it even when it is imputed to his only Son! The cross thunders more terribly than Sinai itself against human sin. How it breaks men's hearts to hear its voice! How it divides men from their sins, even as the voice of the Lord breaks the cedars of Lebanon and rends the rock in pieces! If God smites the perfect One who bears our sin, how will he smite the guilty one who rejects his love?

Let the cross speak again, and what does it say with even louder voice? God loves men and delights in mercy. Though he loves righteousness and hates wickedness, yet he loves the sons of men, so much so that he gives his only Begotten to die that sinners may live. What more could God have done to prove his love to mankind? "God commends his love to us, in that while we were yet sinners, Christ died for us." The love within that glorious deed needs no telling; it tells itself. God had but one Son, one with himself by mystic union, and he sent him here below to take our nature, that, being found in fashion as a man, he might die on our behalf, made sin for us that we might be made the righteousness of God in him. "God so loved the world, that he gave his only begotten Son, that whosoever believes in him might not perish, but have everlasting life." The word of the cross is, "God is love." he wills not the death of the sinner, but that he turn unto him and live.

What next does the cross say? Mark, we are not speaking of the crucifix. The crucifix represents Christ on the cross, but he is not on the cross any longer; he has finished his sacrificial work and has ascended to his glory. If he were still on the cross, he could not save us. We now preach the cross as that on which he died who now lives and reigns, full of ability to save. Let the bare cross speak, and it declares that the one sacrifice is accepted and the atonement is complete. Sin is put away, the work of reconciliation is accomplished, and Jesus has gone up on high unto his Father's throne to plead for the guilty. Christ being raised from the dead dies no more, and death has no more dominion over him. He is risen for our justification, and we are accepted in him.

> No more the bloody spear,
> The cross and nails no more,
> For hell itself shakes at his name,
> And all the heavens adore.

Let the cross speak, and it tells of ransom paid and atonement accepted. The law is magnified, justice is satisfied, mercy is no longer bound by the unsatisfied demands of judgment. "God was in Christ, reconciling the world unto himself, not imputing their trespasses unto them, and has committed unto us the word of reconciliation," which also is the word of the cross.

When we let the cross speak still further, we hear it say, "Come and welcome!" Guilty sons of men, come and welcome to the feast of mercy, for God has both vindicated his law and displayed his love, and now for the chief of sinners there is free and full forgiveness to be had—to be had for nothing, for the cross gives priceless blessings without price. "Whosoever will, let him take the water of life freely." Free pardon, free justification, perfect cleansing, complete salvation, these are gifts of grace bestowed upon the unworthy so soon as they believe in Christ Jesus and trust themselves with him. This is the word of the cross. What more can we desire to hear? We may be forgiven in a way that shall not violate the claims of justice. God is just, and yet the justifier of him that believes. He is merciful and just to forgive us our sins. Oh that I knew how to be quite still and to let the cross itself speak out with its matchless tones of mercy and majesty, love and blood, death and life, punishment and pardon, suffering and glory. It speaks in thunder and in tenderness. If we will but listen to what it has to say, it is a word by which the inmost heart of God is revealed.

Now speak I yet further the word of the cross, for in the name of him who did hang upon the cross I call for faith in his atonement. The death of Christ was no ordinary matter; the dignity of his nature made it the event of the ages. He who died on the cross was very God of very God, as well as man, and his sacrifice is not to be neglected or rejected with impunity. Such a divine marvel demands our careful thought and joyful confidence. To do despite to the blood of the Son of God is to sin with a vengeance. God demands faith in his Son, and especially in his Son dying for our sakes. We ought to believe every word that God has spoken, but above all the word of the cross. Shall we doubt the good faith and love of God when he gives his Son a hostage for his word and offers up the only begotten as the token of his grace? Oh, men, whatever you trifle with, disregard not the Son of God! Whatever presumption you commit, yet trample not upon the cross of Jesus. This is the highest thought of God, the center of all his counsels, the topmost summit of the mighty Alp of divine lovingkindness. Do not think little of it or turn away from it. I beseech you, nay command you, in the name of him who lives and was dead, look to the dying Savior and live. If you do not so, you shall answer for it in that day when he shall come upon the clouds of heaven to avenge him of his adversaries. Thus have I set before you the word of the cross; may the Holy Spirit bless the message.

The Word of Its Despisers

We have the unpleasant task, in the second place, of listening to the word of its despisers. They call the doctrine of the atonement "foolishness." Numbers of men call the doctrine of salvation by the blood of Christ "foolishness." It is most assuredly the wisdom of God and the power of God, but they stick at the first assertion and will not acknowledge the wisdom of the wondrous plan. It is therefore no wonder that they never feel its power. No, it is foolishness to them, a thing beneath their contempt. And why foolishness? "Because," say they, "see how the common people take it up. Everybody can understand it. You believe that Jesus is a substitute for you, and you sing with the poorest of the poor—

> I do believe, I will believe
> That Jesus died for me;
> And on the cross he shed his blood
> From sin to set me free.

"There," say they, "that's a pretty ditty for educated men. Why, the very children sing it, are able to believe it, and talk of it. Psha, it is sheer foolishness!

We don't want anything so vulgar and commonplace. Don't you know that we take in a high-class review and read the best thought of the times? You don't suppose we are going to believe just as common plowboys and servant girls may do?"

Ah me! How mighty wise some people think themselves! Is every truth that can be understood by simple minds to be thrown aside as foolishness? Is nothing worth knowing except the fancy thinking of the select portion of humanity? Are the well-known facts of nature foolishness because they are open to all? Is it quite certain that all the wisdom in the world dwells with the superfine gentlemen who sneer at everything and take in a review? These superficial readers of superior literature, are they the umpires of truth? I wish that their culture had taught them modesty. Those who glorify themselves and sneer at others are usually not wise but otherwise; and those who call other people fools may be looking in the glass and not out of the window. He who is truly wise has some respect for others and the profoundest respect for the Word of God.

But why is it that you count the gospel of the cross to be foolishness? It is this: because this religion of ours, this doctrine of the cross, is not the offspring of reason but the gift of revelation. All the thinkers of the ages continued to think, but they never invented a plan of salvation in which divine justice and mercy should be equally conspicuous. The cross was not in all their thoughts. How could it be? As a thought it originated with the infinite mind and could have originated nowhere else. The doctrine of the cross is not a speculation but a revelation, and for this reason the learned ones cannot endure it. It is God telling men something they could not else have known, and this suits not the profound thinkers who cannot bear to be told anything but must needs think out everything, evolving it from their inner consciousness or from the depths of their vast minds. Now, inasmuch as nothing can come out of a man that is not in him, and as the supreme love of God never was in such an unlovely thing as an unregenerate man, it happens that the doctrine of atonement never originated with man but was taught to him by God at the gates of Eden. The plan that blends vengeance and love was never invented by human imagination. Since man has such an aversion to the great atonement, he could not have been the author of the idea, and he was not the author of it. God alone reveals it in language that babes may understand, and therefore carnal pride calls it "foolishness."

Besides, the carnal man thinks it foolishness because it makes him out to be a fool, and you may take my word for it that anything that proves either you or me to be a fool will at once strike us as being very foolish. Our conscience is dull, and therefore we retaliate upon those who tell us unpleasant truth. "Why, am I nobody after all? I, bound in the best black cloth and wearing a white scarf? So religious and so respectable, so thoughtful, so studious, so profound, am I to be nobody? Do you dare to say to me, 'Except you be converted and become as little children, you shall in no wise enter the kingdom'! My dear sir, you cannot know what you are talking about. Why, I am a professor, a philosopher, a doctor of divinity, and therefore you cannot really mean that I am to receive truth as a little child! Such talk is foolishness." Of course they say so. We always reckoned that they would say so.

I have rejoiced when I have read the skeptical papers and have seen how they sneer at the old-fashioned gospel. The Bible said that carnal men could not receive spiritual things; how truthful is its statement! It is written, "There shall come in the last days scoffers." Here they are, hastening to prove by their conduct the things that they deny. One is grieved that any should scoff, and yet in a measure we are rejoiced to find such confirmation of truth from the lips of her enemies. As long as the world lasts, ungodly men will despise a revelation that they are unable to understand; it is beyond their sphere, and therefore its preachers seem to be babblers and its doctrines to be foolishness.

But, in very deed, it may well seem foolishness to them, for it treats on subjects for which they have no care. If I were able to explain to a general audience how to make unlimited profit upon the stock exchange or in some other market, all the world would listen with profound attention. And if I put my point clearly, I should be pronounced a really clever preacher, a man well worth hearing. But when the sermon is only about the word of God, eternity, the soul, and the blood of Jesus—most people turn on their heel. They are not sure that they have souls, and they refuse to argue upon the supposition of a future existence, which is an old wife's fable to them. As for eternity, their philosophy has no room for it and they do not concern themselves about it. One said in argument the other day, "I believe I shall die like a dog." I could give him no better reply on the spur of the moment than to say, "If I had known that you were a dog, I would have brought you a bone." As I had the notion that he would live forever, I came to talk to him upon subjects suitable to an immortal being, but as I found out that he was going to die like a dog, what could I do for him but provide such cheer as the creature could enjoy?

These men call the gospel foolishness because they look after the main chance and care more for the body than for the soul. One of their wise men said, "Why do you preach so much about the world to come? Why not preach about the world which now is? Teach these people how to ventilate their sewers; that is a much more needful matter than their believing on Jesus." Well, sanitary matters are important, and if any of you feel that you have nothing to live for but ventilating sewers, I wish you would live at a great rate and get it done as quickly as you can. Meanwhile, as we are convinced of the need of other things besides drainage, and as many of us expect soon to take our happy flight to a place where there are no sewers to ventilate, we shall look into those things that concern our future life, seeing they also fit us for the life that now is.

They call the word of the cross foolishness because they regard all the truths with which it deals as insignificant trifles. "Soul!" say they, "What matters whether we have a soul or not? Sin—what is it but the blunder of a poor creature who knows no better?" Of all things, the eternal God is the greatest trifle to unbelieving men. It is merely a name to swear by; that is all. They admit that there may be a great master force in nature or an energy coextensive with the existence of matter, hence they allow theism or pantheism, but they will not endure a personal God whom they are bound to obey. Theism and pantheism are only masks for atheism. These men will have no personal God who loves them and whom they love. God is a nonentity to them, and therefore when we speak of God as real, sin as real, and heaven as real—and God knows they are the only real things—then straightway they mutter, "Foolishness." As for us, we deplore their folly and pray God to teach them better. Having entered by a new birth into the realm of spiritual things, we know the reality and power of the word of the cross.

Now, brothers, I say of these gentlemen who pronounce the gospel foolishness that you need not take much notice of them because they are not capable witnesses; they are not qualified to form a judgment upon the subject. I do not depreciate their abilities in other respects, but it is certain that a blind man is no judge of colors, a deaf man is no judge of sound, and a man who has never been quickened into spiritual life can have no judgment as to spiritual things. How can he? I, for instance, have felt the power of the gospel, and I assert that I have done so. Another man declares that I am not speaking the truth. Why not? Because he has not himself felt that power. Is that sound reasoning?

Have you not heard of the Irishman who, when five men swore that they saw him commit a theft, made answer that he could produce fifty people who did not see him do it. Would there have been any force in that negative evidence? And what if all the world except two men should say, "We do not feel the power of the cross"? Would that be any evidence against the fact asserted by the two? I think not. Two honest men who witness to a fact are to be believed, even though twenty thousand persons are unable to bear such witness. The unspiritual are incapable witnesses; they put themselves out of court, for at the outset they assert that they are not cognizant of those things concerning which we bear testimony. Their assertion is that they never were the subjects of spiritual influences, and we quite believe what they say. But we do not believe them when they go further and assert that therefore what we have seen, tasted, and handled is all a delusion. Concerning that matter they are not capable witnesses.

And I beg you to notice that those who call the gospel of the cross folly are themselves, if rightly looked at, proofs of their own folly and of the sad results of unbelief. The Christians in Paul's days felt that the gospel had emancipated them from the bondage of idolatry and vice, and when they heard others that were captives under these delusions telling them that the emancipating force was foolishness, they looked at them and smiled at the absurdity of the statement. They noticed that such men were them-selves perishing. What a calamity it is for a man to be perishing! A house is unoccupied, its floor is untrod-den, its hearth knows no genial glow. It suffers from neglect; it is perishing. Men who are not living to God are missing the end of their being and like deserted houses are falling into ruin; they are perishing. While unoccupied by good, such minds are surrounded by powers of evil.

Yonder is a tree, I have seen many such—around its trunk the ivy has twisted itself, grasping it like a huge python and crushing it in its folds. The tree is perishing; its very life is being sucked out by the parasite that grasps it. Multitudes of men have about them lusts and sins and errors that are eating out their life—they are perishing. Their souls and char-acters are as timber devoured by dry rot; it remains in the fabric of the house, but it is perishing. Ungodly men are devoured by their own pride, eaten up by self-confidence. Unbelieving men are comparable to a ship drifting to destruction: it has snapped its cable, it is nearing the rocks, it will be broken to pieces, it is perishing! Those who believe not in Jesus are drifting towards a sure immortality of misery. They are daily perishing, and yet while they perish they condemn the means of rescue.

Fancy drowning mariners mocking at the lifeboat! Imagine a diseased man ridiculing the only remedy. That which we have tried and proved they call "foolishness." We have only to answer them, "You are yourselves, as you remain captives to your sins, the victims of foolishness. You are yourselves, as you waste your lives, as you drift to destruction, proofs that the foolishness is not in the cross but in you that reject it." The preaching of the cross is to them that perish foolishness, but to nobody else. O that their hearts were changed by the power of the word, then would they see all wisdom in the word of the cross.

The Word of Those Who Believe

We come, in the third place, to notice the word of those who believe. What do they say of the cross? They call it power, the power of God. The more we study the gospel, the more we are surprised at the singular display of wisdom it contains; but we will not say much upon that point, for we are not qualified to be judges of wisdom. But we do say this: the word of the cross is power. It has been the power of God to us; it has worked upon us as nothing else has ever done. Its work upon many of us has been so remarkable that even onlookers must have been surprised at it.

The phenomenon of conversion is a fact. Men and women are totally changed, and the whole manner of their life is altered. It is of no use to deny the fact, for instances of it come before us every day: unbelievers become devout, the immoral become pure, the dishonest become upright, the blasphemous become gracious, the unchaste become holy. Evil ways are on a sudden deserted, and penitents struggle toward virtue. We see persons in all ranks of society undergoing a radical transformation—self-satisfied people are humbled by the discovery of their unworthiness, and others who were steeped in immorality renounce their vicious pleasures and seek happiness in the service of God.

How do you account for this? We who are the subjects of such a change account for it in this way—it is wrought by the doctrine of the cross, and the power that accomplishes the change is the power of God. No force less than divine could have effected so great a change. The word of the cross has delivered us from the love of sin. No sin is now our master; we have broken every fetter of evil habit. We fall into sin, but we mourn over it, hate the sin, and hate ourselves for committing it. We have been clean delivered from the bondage of corruption and made free to serve the Lord. We have also been delivered from the dread that once bowed us down, a horrible dread that held us in bondage and made us tremble before our Father and our Friend. We thought hardly of God and fled from him; from this we are now delivered, for now we love him and delight in him, and the nearer we can approach him the happier we are.

We have been delivered, also, from the power of Satan. That evil prince has great power over men, and once we were led captive at his will. Even now he attacks us, but we overcome him through the blood of the Lamb. We are also daily delivered from self and from the world, and from all things that would enthrall us. We are being saved; yea, we are saved. Every day a saving force is operating upon us to set us free from the thralldom of corruption. This we feel and know. We are bound for the kingdom, and nothing can keep us back. We are bound for purity, for ultimate perfection. We feel eternal life within us, urging us upward and onward, beyond ourselves and our surroundings. We sit here like eagles chained to the rock by the feebleness of our bodies, but the aspiration within us tells us that we are born to soar among pure and glorified spirits.

We feel that heaven is born within us, born by the word of the cross through the Spirit. We could tell the histories of some here present, or, better still, they could tell them themselves, histories of changes sudden but complete, marvelous but enduring, changes from darkness to light, from death to life. How gladly could we detain you with details of our being upheld when our temptations have been almost overwhelming and kept pressing forward in Christ's service when we had been altogether without strength had not the word of the cross poured new energy into us. We have been ready to die in despair until we have looked to the cross, and then the clouds have yielded to clear shining. A sight of the bleeding Savior and a touch of his hand have made us men again, and we have lifted up our heads as from among the dead. Under the power of the cross we still advance from strength to strength. There is power in the word of the cross to make a man grow into something nobler than he ever dreamed of. We shall not know what we shall be till we shall see our Lord and Savior as he is.

Why, brothers, the power with which God created the world was no greater than the power with which he made us new men in Christ Jesus. The power with which he sustains the world is not greater than the power by which he sustains his people under trial and temptation. And even the raising of the dead at the end of the world will be no greater display of divine power than the raising of dead souls out of their spiritual graves. These wonders of power are being performed in our own experience every day of the week, entirely through the cross. I appeal to you who are truly converted, were you converted through the wisdom of man? I appeal to you that are kept from sinning, are you led towards holiness by the power of elocution, of rhetoric, or of logic? I appeal to you who are despairing, are you ever revived by musical words and rhythmical sentences? Or do you owe all to Jesus crucified?

What is your life, my brothers, but the cross? Whence comes the bread of your soul but from the cross? What is your joy but the cross? What is your delight, what is your heaven, but the Blessed One, once crucified for you, who ever lives to make intercession for you? Cling to the cross, then. Put both arms around it! Hold to the Crucified, and never let him go. Come afresh to the cross at this moment and rest there now and forever! Then, with the power of God resting upon you, go forth and preach the cross! Tell out the story of the bleeding Lamb. Repeat the wondrous tale, and nothing else. Never mind how you do it, only proclaim that Jesus died for sinners. The cross held up by a babe's hand is just as powerful as if a giant held it up. The power lies in the word itself, or rather in the Holy Spirit who works by it and with it.

Brothers, believe in the power of the cross for the conversion of those around you. Do not say of any man that he cannot be saved. The blood of Jesus is omnipotent. Do not say of any district that it is too sunken, or of any class of men that they are too far gone; the word of the cross reclaims the lost. Believe it to be the power of God, and you shall find it so. Believe in Christ crucified and preach boldly in his name, and you shall see great things and gladsome things. Do not doubt the ultimate triumph of Christianity. Do not let a mistrust flit across your soul. The cross must conquer; it must blossom with a crown, a crown commensurate with the person of the Crucified and the bitterness of his agony. His reward shall parallel his sorrows. Trust in God, lift your banner high, and now with psalms and songs advance to battle, for the Lord of hosts is with us, the Son of the Highest leads our van. Onward, with blast of silver trumpet and shout of those who seize the spoil. Let no man's heart fail him! Christ has died! Atonement is complete! God is satisfied! Peace is proclaimed! Heaven glitters with proofs of mercy already bestowed upon ten thousand times ten thousand! Hell is trembling, heaven adoring, earth waiting. Advance, you saints, to certain victory! You shall overcome through the blood of the Lamb.

The Man of One Subject[19]

"For I determined not to know any thing among you, save Jesus Christ, and him crucified."
(1 Corinthians 2:2)

Paul was a very determined man, and whatever he undertook he carried out with all his heart. Once let him say "I determined," and you might be sure of a vigorous course of action. "This one thing I do" was always his motto. The unity of his soul and its mighty resoluteness were the main features of his

---

19. Published in *Metropolitan Tabernacle Pulpit*, Vol. 21 in 1875 by Charles Spurgeon. This is sermon 1264, delivered on October 31, 1875.

character. He had once been a great opposer of Christ and his cross and had shown his opposition by furious persecutions. It was not so very much to be wondered at that when he became a disciple of this same Jesus, whom he had persecuted, he should become a very ardent one and bring all his faculties to bear upon the preaching of Christ crucified. His conversion was so marked, so complete, so thorough that you expect to see him as energetic for the truth as once he had been violent against it.

A man so wholehearted as Paul, so thoroughly capable of concentrating all his forces as the apostle was and so entirely won over to the faith of Jesus, was likely to enter into his cause with all his heart and soul and might and determine to know nothing else but his crucified Lord. Yet do not think that the apostle was a man easily absorbed in one thought. He was, above the most of men, a reasoner, calm, judicious, candid, and prudent. He looked at things in their bearings and relations and was not a stickler for minor matters.

Perhaps even more than might perfectly be justified, he made himself all things to all men that he might by all means win some, and therefore any determination he came to was only arrived at after taking counsel with wisdom. He was not a zealot of that class that may be likened to a bull that shuts its eyes and runs straight forward, seeing nothing that may lie to the right or to the left. He looked all round him calmly and quietly, and though he did in the end push forward in a direct line at his one object, yet it was with his eyes wide open, perfectly knowing what he was doing and believing that he was doing the best and wisest thing for the cause he desired to promote. If, for instance, to have opened his ministry at Corinth by proclaiming the unity of the Godhead or by philosophically working out the possibilities of God's becoming incarnate—if these had been the wisest plans for spreading the Redeemer's kingdom, Paul would have adopted them. But he looked at them all, and having examined them with all care, he could not see that anything was to be gotten by indirect preaching or by keeping back a part of the truth, and therefore he determined to go straight forward and promote the gospel by proclaiming the gospel.

Whether men would hear or whether they would forbear, he resolved to come to the point at once and preach the cross in its naked simplicity. Instead of knowing a great many things that might have led up to the main subject, he would not know anything in Corinth save Jesus Christ, and him crucified. Paul might have said, "I had better beat about the bush and educate the people up to a certain mark before I come to my main point; to lay bare my ultimate intent at the first might be to spread the net in the sight of the birds and frighten them away. I will be cautious and reticent and will take them with guile, enticing them on in pursuit of truth." But not so. Looking at the matter all round as a prudent man should, he comes to this resolve: that he will know nothing among them save Jesus Christ and him crucified.

I would to God that the "culture" we hear of in these days and all this boasted "modern thought" would come to the same conclusion. This most renowned and scholarly divine, after reading, marking, learning, and inwardly digesting everything as few men could do, yet came to this as to the issue of it all: "I determined not to know anything among you, save Jesus Christ, and him crucified." May God grant that the critical skill of our contemporaries and their laborious excogitations may land them on the same shore by the blessing of the Holy Spirit.

What Was Paul's Subject at Corinth?

Our first consideration this morning will be, what was this subject to which Paul determined to shut himself up while preaching to the church at Corinth? That subject was one, though it may also be divided into two: it was the person and the work of our Lord Jesus Christ, laying special stress upon that part of his work that is always the most objected to, namely, his substitutionary sacrifice, his redeeming death. Paul preached Christ in all his positions, but he especially dwelt upon him as the crucified one.

The apostle first preached his great Master's person—Jesus Christ. There was no equivocation about Paul when he spoke of Jesus of Nazareth. He held him up as a real man, no phantom, but one who was crucified, dead and buried, and rose again from the dead in actual bodily existence. There was no hesitation about his Godhead either. Paul preached Jesus as the Son of the Highest, as the wisdom and the power of God, as one "in whom dwells all the fullness of the Godhead bodily." You never doubted when you heard Paul but that he believed in the divinity and the humanity of the Lord Jesus Christ and worshiped and adored him as very God of very God. He preached his person with all clearness of language and warmth of love. The Christ of God was all in all to Paul.

The apostle spoke equally clearly upon the Redeemer's work, especially laying stress upon his death. "Horrible!" said the Jew, "How can you boast in a man who died a felon's death and was cursed because he was hanged on a tree!"

"Ah," said the Greek, "tell us no more about your God that died! Babble no longer about resurrection. We never shall believe such unmitigated foolishness."

But Paul did not, therefore, put these things into the background and say, "Gentlemen, I will begin with telling you of the life of Christ and of the excellency of his example, and by this means I shall hope to tempt you onward to the conclusion that there was something divine in him and then afterwards to the further conclusion that he made an atonement for sin."

But no, he began with his blessed person and distinctly described him as he had been taught by the Holy Spirit, and as to his crucifixion he put it in the front and made it the main point. He did not say, "Well, we will leave the matter of his death for a time," or "We will consider it under the aspect of a martyrdom by which he completed his testimony," but he gloried in the crucified Redeemer, the dead and buried Christ, the sin-bearing Christ, the Christ made a curse for us, as it is written, "Cursed is every one that hangs on a tree." This was the subject to which he confined himself at Corinth; beyond this he would not stir an inch. Nay, he does not merely determine to keep his preaching to that point, but he resolves not even to know any other subject; he would keep his mind fast closed among them to any thought but Jesus Christ and him crucified.

Very impolitic this must have seemed. Call in a council of worldly wise men, and they will condemn such a rash course. For in the first place such preaching would drive away all the Jews. Holding as the Jews did the Old Testament Scriptures, and receiving therefore a great deal of teaching about the Messiah, and holding very firmly to the unity of the Godhead, the Jews had gone a long way towards the light, and if Paul had kept back the objectionable points a little while, might he not have drawn them a little further and so by degrees have landed them at the cross? Wise men would have remarked upon the hopefulness of the Israelites, if handled with discretion, and their advice would have been, "We do not say, renounce your sentiments, Paul, but disguise them for a little while. Do not say what is untrue, but at the same time be a little reticent about what is true, or else you will drive away these hopeful Jews."

The apostle yielded to no such policy; he would not win either Jew or Gentile by keeping back the truth, for he knew that such converts are worthless. If the man who is near the kingdom will be driven right away from the gospel by hearing the unvarnished truth, that is no guide as to Paul's duty. He knows that the gospel must be a "savor of death unto death" to some as well as of "life unto life" unto others, and therefore whichever may occur he must deliver his own soul. Consequences are not for him, but for the Lord. It is ours to speak the truth boldly, and in every case we shall be a sweet savor unto God; but to temper in the hope of making converts is to do evil that good may come, and this is never to be thought of for an instant.

Another would say "But, Paul, if you do this you will arouse opposition. Do you not know that Christ crucified is a byword and a reproach to all thinking men? Why, at Corinth there are a number of philosophers, and I tell you it will create unbounded ridicule if you so much as open your mouth about the Crucified One and his resurrection. Do not you remember on Mars Hill how they mocked you when you spoke upon that theme? Do not provoke their contempt. Argue with their Gnosticism and show them that you too are a philosopher. Be all things to all men; be learned among the learned and rhetorical among the orators. By these means you will make many friends, and by degrees your conciliatory conduct will bring them to accept the gospel."

The apostle shakes his head, puts down his foot, and with firm voice utters his decision, "I have determined," says he, "I have already made up my mind. Your counsels and advice are lost upon me; I have determined to know nothing among the Corinthians, however learned the Gentile portion of them may be or however fond of rhetoric, save Jesus Christ and him crucified." He stands to that.

It is further worthy of note that the apostle had resolved that his subject should so engross the attention of his hearers that he would not even speak it with excellency of speech or garnish it with man's wisdom. You have heard perhaps of the famous painter who drew the likeness of James I. He represented him sitting in a bower with all the flowers of the season blooming around him, and nobody ever took the smallest notice of the king's visage, for all eyes were charmed by the excellency of the flowers. Paul resolved that he would have no flowers at all, that the portrait he sketched should be Christ crucified, the bare fact and doctrine of the cross without so much as a single flower from the poets or the philosophers. Some of us need not be very loud in our resolution to avoid fine speech, for we may have but slender gifts in that direction, but the apostle was a man of fine natural powers and of vast attainments, a man whom the Corinthian critics could not have despised, and yet he threw away all ornaments to let the unadorned beauty of the cross win its own way.

As he would not add flowers, so he would not darken the cross with smoke, for there is a way of preaching the gospel amid a smother of mystification and doubt, so that men cannot perceive it. A numerous band of men are always boiling and stirring up a huge philosophic caldron, which steams with dense vapor, beclouding the cross of Christ most horribly. Alas for that wisdom that conceals the wisdom of God—it is the most guilty form of folly. Some people preach Christ as I have seen representations of a man-of-war in battle. The painter painted nothing but the smoke, and you have said, "Where is the ship?" Well, if you looked long you might discern a fragment of the top of one of the masts and, perhaps, a portion of the boom; the ship was there, no doubt, but the smoke concealed it.

So there may be Christ in some men's preaching, but there is such a cloud of thinking, such a dense pall of profundity, such a horrid smoke of philosophy, that you cannot see the Lord. Paul painted beneath a clear sky; he would have no learned obscurity. He determined not to know how to speak after the manner of the orators, not to know how to think deeply according to the mode of the philosophers but only to know Jesus Christ and him crucified, and just to set him forth in his own natural beauties unadorned. He dispensed with those accessories that are so apt to attract the eye of the mind from the central point—Christ crucified.

"A rash experiment," says one. Ah, Brothers, it is the experiment of faith, and faith is justified of all her children. If we rely upon the power of mere persuasion, we rely upon that which is born of the flesh. If we depend upon the power of logical argument, we again rely upon that which is born of men's reason. If we trust to poetic expressions and attractive turns of speech, we look to carnal means. But if we rest upon the naked omnipotence of a crucified Savior, upon the innate power of the wondrous deed of love that was consummated upon Calvary, and believe that the Spirit of God will make this the instrument for the conversion of men, the experiment cannot possibly end in failure.

But oh, my brothers, what a task this must have been for Paul! He was not like some of us, who are neither familiar with philosophy nor capable of oratory. He was so great a master of both that he must have found it needful to keep himself constantly in check. I think I can see him every now and then when a deeply intellectual thought has come across his mind and a beautiful mode of utterance has suggested itself, reining himself up and saying to his mind, "I will leave these deep thoughts for the Romans. I will give them all this in the eighth chapter. But as for these Corinthians, they shall have nothing but Christ crucified, for they are so carnal, so grossly slavish before talent that they will run away with the idea that my excellent way of putting the truth was the power of it. They shall have Christ only, and only Christ. They are children, and I must speak to them as such. They are mere babes in Christ and have need of milk, and milk alone must I give them. They claim to be clever and learned, but they are conceited, high-minded, full of divisions and controversies. I will give them nothing but 'the old, old story of Jesus and his love,' and I will tell them that story simply as to a little child." Boundless love to their souls thus made him concentrate his testimony upon the one central point of Jesus crucified. Thus I have shown you what his subject was.

The Testimony Was Sufficient for His Purpose

Now, secondly, although Paul thus concentrated his energies upon one point of testimony, it was quite sufficient for his purpose. If the apostle had aimed at pleasing an intelligent audience, Christ and him crucified would not have done at all. If again he had designed to set himself up as a profound teacher, he would naturally have looked out for something new, something a little more dazzling than the person and work of the Redeemer. And if Paul had desired, as I am afraid some of my brothers do, to collect together a class of highly independent minds—which is I believe the euphemism for freethinkers—to draw together a select church of the men of culture and intellect—which generally means a club of men who despise the gospel—he certainly would not have kept to preaching Jesus Christ and him crucified. This order of men would deny him all hope of success with such a theme. They would assure him that such preaching would only attract the poorer sort and the less educated, the servant maids and the old women. But Paul would not have been disconcerted by such observations, for he loved the souls of the poorest and feeblest, and besides, he knew that what had exercised power over his own educated mind was likely to have power over other intelligent people, and so he kept to the doctrine of the cross, believing that he had therein an instrument that would effectually accomplish his one design with all classes of men.

Brothers, what did Paul wish to do? Paul desired first of all to arouse sinners to a sense of sin, and what has ever accomplished this so perfectly as the doctrine that sin was laid upon Christ and caused his death? The sinner, enlightened by the Holy Spirit, sees at once that sin is not a trifle, that it is not to be forgiven without an atonement but must be followed by penalty, borne by someone or other. When the guilty one has seen the Son of God bleeding to death in pangs unutterable in consequence of sin, he has learned that sin is an enormous and crushing burden. If even the Son of God cries out beneath it, if his death agony rends the heavens and shakes the earth, what an awful evil sin must be. What must it involve upon my soul if in my own person I shall be doomed to bear its consequences? Thus the sinner rightly argues, and thus is he aroused to a sense of guilt.

But Paul wanted also to awaken in the minds of the guilty that humble hope that is the great instrument of leading men to Jesus. He desired to make them hope that forgiveness might be given consistently with justice. Oh, brothers, Christ crucified is the one ray of light that can penetrate the thick darkness of despair and make a penitent heart hope for pardon from the righteous Judge. Need a sinner ever doubt when he has once seen Jesus crucified? When he understands that there is pardon for every transgression through the bleeding wounds of Jesus, is not the best form of hope at once kindled in his bosom, and is he not led to say, "I will arise and go unto my Father, and will say unto him, 'Father, I have sinned'"?

Paul longed yet further to lead men to actual faith in Jesus Christ. Now, faith in Jesus Christ can only come by preaching Jesus Christ. Faith comes by hearing, but the hearing must be upon the subject concerning which the faith is to deal. If you would make believers in Christ, preach Christ. The things of Christ, applied by the Spirit, lead men to put their reliance upon Christ. Nor was that all. Paul wanted men to forsake their sins, and what should lead them to hate evil so much as seeing the sufferings of Jesus on account of it? You and I know the power of a bleeding Savior to make us take revenge upon sin. What indignation, what searching of heart, what stern resolve, what bitterness of regret, what deep repentance have we felt when we have seen that our sins became the nails, the hammer, the spear, yea, the executioners of the Well-Beloved?

And Paul longed to train up in Corinth a church of consecrated men, full of love, full of self-denial, a holy people, zealous for good works. And let me ask you, what more is there necessary to preach to any man to promote his sanctification and his consecration than Jesus Christ, who has redeemed us and so made us forever his servants? What argument is stronger than the fact that we are not our own, for we are bought with a price?

I say that Paul had in Christ crucified a subject equal to his object, a subject that would meet the case of every man however degraded or however cultured and a subject that would be useful to men in the first hours of the new birth and equally useful when they were made meet to be partakers of the inheritance of the saints in light. He had a subject for today and tomorrow and a subject for next year, for Jesus Christ is the same yesterday, today, and forever. He had in the crucified Jesus a subject for the prince's palace and a subject for the peasant's hut, a subject for the market-place and a subject for the academy, for the heathen temple and for the synagogue. Wherever he might go, Christ would be both to Jew and Gentile, to bond and free, the wisdom of God and the power of God, and that not to one form of beneficial influence alone but unto full salvation to everyone that believes.

Confining Himself to Christ Could Not Do Harm

But I must pass on to a third remark, that the apostle's confining himself to this subject could not possibly do harm. You know, brothers, that when men dwell exclusively upon one thing, they get pretty strong there, but they generally become very weak in other points. Hence a man of one thought only is generally described as riding a hobby. Well, this was Paul's hobby, but it was a sort of hobby a man may ride without any injury to himself or his neighbor; he will be none the less a complete man if he surrenders himself wholly and only to this one theme.

But let me remark that Christ crucified is the only subject of which this can be said. Let me show you that it is so. You know a class of ministers who preach doctrine and doctrine only. Their mode of preaching resembles the counting of your fingers: "one, two, three, four, five," and for a variety, "five, four, three two, one"—always a certain set of great truths and no others. What is the effect of this ministry? Well, generally to breed a generation of men who think they know everything but really do not know much. Very decided, and so far good; but very narrow, very exclusive, very bigoted, and so far bad. You cannot preach doctrine alone without contracting your own mind and that of your hearers.

There are others who preach experience only. They are very good people; I am not condemning either them or their doctrinal friends, but they also fall into mischief. Some of them take the lower scale of experience, and they tell us that nobody can be a child of God except he feels the horrible character of his inbred sin and groans daily, being burdened. We used to hear a good deal of that some years ago; there is less of it now. Am I wrong in saying that this teaching trains up a race of men who show their humility by sitting in judgment upon all who cannot groan down to as deep a note as they can?

Another class has lately arisen who preach experience, but theirs is always upon the high key. They soar aloft, as I think, a little in the balloon line. They own only the bright side of experience; they have nothing to do with its darkness and death. For them there are no nights; they sing through perpetual summer days. They have conquered sin, and they have ignored themselves. So they say, but we should not have thought so if they had not told us so. On the contrary, we might have fancied that they had a very vivid idea of themselves and their own attainments. I hope I am mistaken, but it has appeared to some of us poor fallible beings that in some beloved brothers self had grown marvelously big of late; certainly their conventions and preachings largely consist of very wonderful declarations of their own admirable condition. I should be pleased to learn of their progress in grace, if it be real. But I had sooner have made the discovery myself or have heard it from somebody else besides themselves, for there is an inspired proverb that says; "Let another praise you, and not thine own lips." For my part, if any other man thought it right to praise me, I would rather that he held his tongue, for man-magnifying is a poor business. Let the Lord alone be magnified. I think it is clear that grave faults arise, one of exclusively preaching an inner life instead of preaching Christ, who is the life itself.

Another class of ministers has preached the precepts and little else. We want these men as we want the others—they are all useful and act as antidotes to each other—but their ministries are not complete. If you hear preaching about duty and command, it is very proper; but if it be the one sole theme, the teaching becomes very legal in the long run. And after a while the true gospel that has the power to make us keep the precept gets flung into the background, and the precept is not kept after all. Do, do, do, generally ends in nothing being done.

If a brother were to undertake to preach the ordinances only, like those who are always extolling what they are pleased to call the holy sacraments—well, you know where that teaching goes. It has a tendency towards the southeast, and its chosen line runs across the city of Rome.

Moreover, beloved brother, even if you preach Jesus Christ, you must not keep to any other phase of him but that which Paul took, namely, "him crucified," for under no other aspect may you exclusively regard him. For instance, the preaching of the second advent, which, in its place and proportion, is admirable, has been by some taken out of its place, and made the end-all and be-all of their ministry. That, you see, is not what Paul had selected, and it is not a safe selection. In many cases sheer fanaticism has been the result of exclusively dwelling upon prophecy, and probably more men have gone mad on that subject than on any other religions question.

Whether any man ever could become fanatical about Christ crucified I cannot say. I have never heard of such an instance. Whether a man ever went insane with love to the crucified Redeemer I do not know, but I have never met such a case. If I should ever go mad, I should like it to be in that direction, and I should like to bite a great many more, for what a blessed subject it would be for one to be carried away with, to become unreasonably absorbed in Christ crucified, to have gone out of your senses with faith in Jesus. The fact is, it never can injure the mind; it is a doctrine that may be heard forever and will be always fresh, new, and suitable to the whole of our manhood.

I say that the keeping to this doctrine cannot do hurt, and the reason is this: it contains all that is vital within itself. Keep within the limit of Christ and him crucified, and you have brought before men all the essentials for this life and for the life to come; you have given them the root out of which may grow both branch and flower, and fruit of holy thought and word and deed. Let a man know Christ crucified, and he knows him whom to know is life eternal. This is a subject that does not arouse one part of the man and send the other part to sleep; it does not kindle his imagination and leave his judgment uninstructed, nor feed his intellect and starve his heart. There is not a faculty of our nature but what Christ crucified affects for good. The perfect manhood of Christ crucified affects mind, heart, memory, imagination, thought, everything. As in milk there are all the ingredients necessary for sustaining life, so in Christ crucified there is everything that is wanted to nurture the soul. Even as the hand of David's chief minstrel touched every chord of his ten-stringed harp, so Jesus brings sweet music out of our entire manhood.

There is also this to be said about preaching Christ exclusively: that it will never produce animosities. It will not impregnate men's minds with questions and contentions, as those nice points do that some are so fond of dealing with. When certain questions are settled by my judgment and by your judgment, and by a third and a fourth man's judgment, a contest is sure to ensue. But he who stands at Christ's cross and keeps there, stands where he may embrace the whole brotherhood of true Christians, for we are perfectly joined together in one mind and judgment there. There is no vaunting of man's judgment at the cross. "I am of Paul, I am of Apollos, I am of Christ" comes from not keeping to Jesus crucified. But if we keep to the cross as guilty sinners needing cleansing through the precious blood, and finding all our salvation there, we shall not have time to set ourselves up as religious leaders and to cause divisions in the church of Christ. Was there ever yet a sect created in Christendom by the preaching of Christ crucified? No, my brothers, sects are created by the preaching of something over and above this, but this is the soul and marrow of Christianity and consequently the perfect bond of love that holds Christians together.

We Must All Make Christ Crucified the Main Subject of Our Thoughts, Preaching, and Efforts

I shall not say more, but pass on to my last reflection, which is this: Because, then, Paul made this his one sole subject among the Corinthians, and he did no hurt by so doing, which cannot be said of any other subject, I commend to you that we should all of us make this the main subject of our thoughts, preaching, and efforts.

Unconverted men and women, to you I speak first. To you I have nothing else to preach but Jesus Christ and him crucified. Paul knew there were great sinners at Corinth, for it was common all over the then world to call a licentious man a Corinthian. They were a people who pushed laxity and lasciviousness of manners to the greatest possible excess, yet among them Paul knew nothing but Christ and him crucified, because all that the greatest sinner can possibly want is to be found there.

You have nothing in yourself, sinner, and you need not wish for anything to carry to Jesus. You tell me you know nothing about the profound doctrines of the gospel; you need not know them when coming to Christ. The one thing you need to know is this: Jesus Christ, the Son of God, came into the world to save sinners, and whosoever believes in him shall not perish but have everlasting life. I shall be glad for you to be further instructed in the fait, and to know the heights and depths of that love that passes knowledge, but just now the one thing you require to know is Jesus Christ crucified, and if you never get beyond that, if your mind should be of so feeble a cast that anything deeper than this you should never be able to grasp, I for one shall feel no distress whatever, for you will have found that which will deliver you from the power of sin and from the punishment of it and that which will take you up to heaven to dwell where that same Jesus who was crucified sits enthroned at the right hand of God. Oh, dear broken heart, if you would find healing, it is in those wounds. If you would find rest, you must have it from those pierced hands. If you would hear absolution, it must be spoken from those same lips that said so sweetly, "It is finished." God forbid that we should know anything among sinners except Christ and him crucified. Look to him, and him only, and you shall find rest unto your souls.

As for you, my brothers and sisters who know Christ, I have this to say to you: keep this to the front, and nothing else but this, for it is against this that the enemy rages. That part of the line of battle that is most fiercely assailed by the enemy is sure to be that which he knows to be most important to carry. Men hate those they fear. The antagonism of the enemies of the gospel is mainly against the cross. From the very first it was so. They cried "Let him come down from the cross and we will believe in him." They will write us pretty lives of Christ and tell us what an excellent man he was and do our Lord such homage as their Judas's lips can afford him. They will also take his Sermon on the Mount and say what a wonderful insight he had into the human heart, and what a splendid code of morals he taught, and so on. "We will be Christians" say they, "but the dogma of atonement we utterly reject."

Our answer is: we do not care one farthing what they have to say about our Master if they deny his substitutionary sacrifice; whether they give him wine or vinegar is a small question so long as they reject the claims of the Crucified. The praises of unbelievers are sickening; who wants to hear polluted lips lauding him? Such sugared words are very like those that came out of the mouth of the devil when he said, "you Son of the Highest," and Jesus rebuked him and said "Hold your peace, and come out of him." Even thus would we say to unbelievers who extol Christ's life: "Hold your peace! We know your enmity, disguise it as you may. Jesus is the Savior of men or he is nothing; if you will not have Christ crucified, you cannot have him at all."

My brothers in Jesus let us glory in the blood of Jesus, let it be conspicuous as though it were sprinkled upon the lintel and the two side posts of our doors, and let the world know that redemption by blood is written upon the innermost tablets of our hearts.

Brothers, this is the test point of every teacher. When a fish goes bad, they say it first stinks at the head, and certainly when a preacher becomes heretical it is always about Christ. If he is not clear about Jesus crucified and you hear one sermon from him—that is your misfortune. But if you go and hear him again, and hear another like the first, it will be your fault. Go a third time, and it will be your crime. If any man be doubtful about Christ crucified, recollect Hart's couplet, for it is a truth: "You cannot be right in the rest. Unless you think rightly of him."

I do not want to examine men upon all the doctrines of the Westminster Assembly's Confession. I begin here, "What think you of Christ?" If you cannot answer that question, go and publish your own views where you like, but you and I are wide as the poles asunder; neither do I wish to have fellowship with you. We must have plain speaking here.

It is Christ crucified that God blesses to conversion. God blessed William Huntingdon to the conversion of souls. I am sure of that, though I am no Huntingdonian. He blessed John Wesley to the conversion of souls. I am quite as clear about that, though I am not a Wesleyan. The point upon which the Lord blessed them both was that wherein they bore testimony to Christ, and you shall find that in proportion as Jesus Christ's atonement is in a sermon, it is the lifeblood of that sermon and is that which God sanctifies to the conversion of the sons of men. Therefore, keep it always prominent.

And I ask you now, my brothers, one thing more, is not Christ and him crucified the thing to live on and the thing to die on? Worldlings can live upon their flimsies; they can delight themselves under their Jonah's gourds while they last. But when a man is depressed in spirit and tortured in body, where does he look? If he be a Christian, where does he fly? Where, indeed, but to Jesus crucified? How often have I been glad to creep into the temple and stand in the poor publican's shoes and say, "God be merciful to me a sinner," looking only to that mercy seat Jesus sprinkled with his precious blood. This will do to die with.

I do not believe we shall die seeking consolation from our peculiar church organizations, nor shall we die grasping with a dying clutch either ordinance or doctrine by itself. Our soul must live and die on Jesus crucified. Notice all the saints when they die whether they do not get back to Calvary's great sacrifice. They believed a great many things; some of them had many crotchets and whims and oddities, but the main point comes uppermost in death. "Jesus died for me; Jesus died for me"—they all come to that. Well, where they get at last, do you not think it would be well to go at first? And if that be the bottom of it all, and it certainly is, would it not be as well for us to keep to that? While some are glorying in this and some in that, some have this form of worship and some that, let us say, "God forbid that I should glory save in the cross of our Lord Jesus Christ, by whom the world is crucified to me and I unto the world."

Brothers, I commend to you more and more the bringing of the cross of Christ into prominence, because it is this that will weld us more and more closely to one another and will keep us in blessed unity. We cannot all understand those peculiar truths that depend very much upon nice points and shades of meaning in the Greek, which only critics can bring out. If you are going in for these pretty things, brother, you must leave behind many of us poor fools, for we cannot go in for these things and you only puzzle us. I know you have that dainty point very beautifully in your own mind, and you think a great deal of it, and I do not wonder, for it has cost you a good deal of thinking and shows your powerful discernment. At the same time, do you not think you ought to condescend to some of us who never will as long as ever we live take up with these knotty points? Some of our brains are of an ordinary sort. We have to earn our bread and we mingle with ordinary people; we know that twice two will make four, but we are not acquainted with all the recondite principles that lie concealed in the lofty philosophy to which you have climbed.

I do not know much about it, I do not climb to such elevations myself, and I shall never get up there along with you. Might it not be better for the unity of the faith that you would kindly leave some of these things alone, agree better with your friends at home, show more love to your fellow Christians, and attend a little more to commonplace duties? I do not know but what it might do you good, and bring a little of your humility to the front, if you kept down there with Jesus Christ and him crucified.

Personally, I might know a host of things—I specially might, for everybody tries to teach me something. I get advice by the wagonload; one pulls this ear and one pulls that. Well, I might know a great deal, but I find I should have to leave some of you behind if I went off to these things, and I love you too well for that. I am determined to know nothing among you but Jesus Christ and him crucified. If any man will keep to that, I will say, "Give me your hand, my brother. Jesus washed it with his blood as he did mine. Come, brother, let us look up together at the same cross. What do you make of it?"

There is a tear in your eye, and there is one in mine, but yet there is a flush of joy upon both our faces because of the dear love that nailed Jesus there. "What shall we do in the sight of this cross?" My brother says, "I will go and win souls," and I say, "So will I." He says, "I have one way of speaking," and I reply, "I have another, for our gifts differ, but we will never clash, for we are serving one Lord and one Master, and we will not be divided, either in this world or in that which is to come."

Let Apollos say what he likes, or Paul or Peter, we will learn from them all and be very glad to do so, but still from the cross we will not move but stand fast there, for Jesus is the first and the last, the Alpha and the Omega. Amen.